TO:

....

FROM:

....

A cross sits atop a hill overlooking a World Vision irrigation project in Morulem, Kenya, that has transformed the Turkana desert into rich farmland.

HE WALKS

ENCOUNTERS WITH CHRIST IN A BROKEN WORLD

AMONG US

RICHARD AND RENEÉ STEARNS

PHOTOGRAPHY BY JON WARREN

COUNTRYMAN

A Division of Thomas Nelson Publishers

THOMAS NELSON

Since 1798

NASHVILLE   DALLAS   MEXICO CITY   RIO DE JANEIRO

Published in Nashville, Tennessee, by Thomas Nelson. Thomas Nelson is a registered trademark of Thomas Nelson, Inc.

Images © 2013 by World Vision, Inc. All rights reserved.

Cover image: Children walk several miles to their village in northern Ghana after collecting water from a crocodile-infested pond.

Authors are represented by the literary agency of Alive Communications, Inc., 7680 Goddard Street, Suite 200, Colorado Springs, CO 80920, www.alivecommunications.com.

Thomas Nelson, Inc., titles may be purchased in bulk for educational, business, fund-raising, or sales promotional use. For information, please e-mail SpecialMarkets@ThomasNelson.com.

Cover and interior design by Faceout Studio, Bend, OR, www.faceoutstudio.com.

ISBN-13: 978-1-4003-2186-5

Printed in China

13 14 15 16 WAI 5 4 3 2 1

www.thomasnelson.com

To all the men and women, boys and girls,

who have trusted us to tell their stories to the world,

the ones Jesus called blessed.

ACKNOWLEDGMENTS

In a very real sense, we are merely eyewitnesses to the incredible stories contained herein. The scores of people featured in this book invited us into their homes and into their lives, sharing their most intimate stories with us, believing that their stories counted for something and that others might benefit from hearing them. So before anyone else we must first acknowledge these courageous men, women, and children. As you might imagine, just finding stories like these across the world is no easy feat. Had it not been for the thousands of World Vision staff who

"They had much to teach us about living, loving, overcoming, and celebrating." —Rich and Reneé Stearns

spend their lives on behalf of the people they serve, we might never have been introduced to those described in these pages. Capturing the narratives required a bucket brigade of collaborators: World Vision's national communications teams, the project workers who daily offer their helping hands, the drivers who took us up mountains and across rivers, and the national staff who planned every aspect of our visits in hope that the telling of these stories might motivate people across the world to care and to get involved.

It also takes a village to prepare a book like this for publication. Lee Hough, our agent, helped us craft our original proposal. The aesthetics of the layout and interior design were achieved by Paul Nielsen from Faceout Studio. At Thomas Nelson, our publishing house, Laura Minchew and Lisa Stilwell helped us shape the look and feel of the book. Jack Countryman gave us the first inspiration to actually attempt a kind of photojournalistic approach to the storytelling.

Inside of World Vision's Seattle office, it took many hands to attend to all of the details. Ashley Day compiled binders filled with hundreds of photos to select from and helped with the captioning. Kari Costanza was our frequent traveling companion and was indispensable in helping find just the right people and stories for us to capture. Milana McLead kept us all focused on the big picture with valuable strategic input. Rob Moll coordinated the editing and proofreading process. And many more have their fingerprints on these pages: Elizabeth Hendley, Jane Sutton-Redner, Denise Koenig, Brian Sytsma, David Shaw, Phil Manzano, Andrea Peer, Laura Reinhardt, Abby Stalsbroten, and Lindsey Minerva.

We are also grateful to family and friends who willingly read our early drafts and who gave us encouragement to plow ahead in this endeavor.

Finally, we are grateful to our God who opened our eyes to see the beauty in the lives of His beloved poor, fearfully and wonderfully made in his image.

RICH AND RENEÉ STEARNS WITH JON WARREN

TABLE OF
CONTENTS

INTRODUCTION

In our years with World Vision, we have logged more than two million air miles traveling to the uttermost parts of the globe. We've been to the heights of the Andes Mountains; navigated rivers like the Zambezi, Mekong, and Rio Negro; traveled across the Rift Valley of Ethiopia and through the jungles of Mozambique; and rambled around the edges of the Gobi and Sahara deserts. But unlike tourists who might travel to these same places just to see the sights and sample the cuisines, we went to meet the people who lived there. We went to listen, to learn, and to offer our hand of friendship. We have been privileged to break bread with these new friends, to hear their incredible stories, and to laugh, cry, and celebrate with them. And when we left, we carried their stories in our hearts.

There is a misunderstanding we often have about the poor—believing that we who have so much are the ones in the position to offer help to those who have so little. But what we have discovered on so many of our trips is that we were the ones who were poor and they were the ones who were rich: rich in wisdom, community, perseverance, courage, faith, and even joy. They had much to teach us about living, loving, overcoming, and celebrating. They had much to teach us about dependence on God.

There is something sacred about their stories. They entrusted their stories to us, believing that we might pass them along, believing that others might benefit not only from their pains and their losses but also from their joys and triumphs. We learned about the power of prayer from Octaviana in Peru, about forgiveness from a young woman named Margaret in Uganda, and about unbounded compassion from Mama Jeanette in the Democratic Republic of the Congo. So we now pass their stories on to you. This devotional anthology is a treasure trove of the people we have met and the deep insights we have gained from them.

Five-year-old Francis flashes a bright smile as her parents partner with volunteers to build the family a new home in Honduras.

Matthew, Mark, Luke, and John told us the stories of people as well—stories in which people encountered Jesus. They told us about Jesus' delight in the widow's mite, the faith of a little boy whose lunch fed five thousand, the men who lowered their crippled friend through a roof believing that Jesus would heal him, and a woman named Mary who lavished her most precious jar of perfume on the feet of Jesus. It is through stories that we, too, encounter Jesus.

Mother Teresa once said that in the faces of the poor, she met "Jesus in His most distressing disguise." We too have met Jesus in the faces of our new friends around the world. And knowing Jesus' great love for "the least of these," is it any wonder that He walks among them?

RICH AND RENEÉ STEARNS, MARCH 2013

FACING GOLIATH

WHATEVER WE ARE FACING, WE CAN REST IN THE ASSURANCE THAT THE OUTCOME DOES NOT DEPEND ON OUR STRENGTH BUT ON GOD'S.

The foolishness of God is wiser than man's wisdom, and the weakness of God is stronger than man's strength.

I CORINTHIANS 1:25

RICHARD WAS THE FIRST. He was the first child I met on my first trip as World Vision's new president. And it was the first time I had ever seen a child who was facing the Goliath we call *poverty.*

I met Richard in the Rakai district of Uganda, where the AIDS crisis was taking away mothers and fathers, leaving children orphaned, and forcing young boys and girls to become heads of households. Richard was thirteen years old and taking care of his two younger brothers. Two crude piles of stones just outside the door of his hut marked the graves of Richard's parents, and he walked past those graves every day. He had buried his mother and father after spending months, maybe years, caring for them as their health declined. He had watched over them as their coughs filled the house, as they became too frail to leave their beds. Richard did his best.

Meeting this young boy, my namesake, was a punch in the stomach, as I had never before seen what poverty does to children. And it was when I first

Around the world, children—this one in Kenya—face many giants.

With more than twenty-three million people living with HIV in sub-Saharan Africa, numerous families—like that of this boy in Kenya—are directly impacted as they face the dual Goliaths of poverty and disease.

began to understand how much the very poor would teach me about life and faith. I asked Richard an awkward question, one that is normally asked of boys and girls who are free to go to school and to dream: "What do you want to be when you grow up?" "A doctor," Richard told me, "so I can help people who have this disease." When I asked about his faith, he ran to get his Bible telling me that he loved to read the book of John, because it speaks of Jesus' love for children. Tears ran down my cheeks as I considered the insurmountable odds this little boy was facing. But Richard was facing his Goliath with both grace and courage.

Another young boy, this one named David, also faced his Goliath with grace and courage: "You come against me with sword and spear and javelin," he said, "but I come against you in the name of the Lord Almighty, the God of the armies of Israel, whom you have defied. This day the Lord will hand you over to me, and I'll strike you down and cut off your head" (1 Samuel 17:45–46). With nothing but a sling, a smooth stone, and faith in the God he served, David slew his Goliath. So, too, Moses challenged a pharaoh and parted the Red Sea with a shepherd's staff. Peter, a simple fisherman, stepped up to lead the early church, and Paul challenged the Roman Empire from his prison cell with nothing but a pen. When people act in God's power, Goliaths fall.

I find great comfort in knowing that God's plan for us does not rely on our greatness, but rather on His. I don't know what Goliath you may be facing, but when your time of testing comes, you can be confident that God will not abandon you. No Goliath you face is mightier than the God you serve. Richard knew that Jesus loved the little children, and that love helped Richard stand strong. You can do the same as you face your Goliaths.

—RICH

LOOSELY HELD

Cling too tightly to what's good, and we just might miss God's best.

No eye has seen, no ear has heard, no mind has conceived what God has prepared for those who love him.

1 Corinthians 2:9

NOT LONG AGO, Rich spoke at a church retreat. During the Q&A session, someone asked how our family had made the decision to leave our old life to follow God's call to World Vision. How did Rich walk away from his corporate career? How did we leave friends, family, home, and community in Pennsylvania and move to Seattle? The way these questions were asked seemed to reflect a bias on the part of the questioner that whatever it was we left behind was probably better than what we found when we got here.

These questions remind me of yet another question, one we asked of a little boy we met in Malawi. Stopping in a village, we found our vehicle immediately surrounded by children. Several had been playing a game of soccer just minutes before, and one boy approached with the soccer ball still in hand. I say soccer ball, but what the child carried was little more than a bundle of old plastic bags tied up with string.

"Can we trade?" we asked. "If we give you a brand-new soccer ball, will you give us yours?" We thought the ball would be a great example of childhood creativity, of how play can triumph over limited resources. For a minute the boy was puzzled, but then he realized that this trade would mean giving up the ball he already owned. He ran back to his buddies to discuss the offer, and only when all had weighed in on the matter did he hand over his homemade ball for the shiny, new white one emblazoned with a swoosh.

It must have been difficult for the little boy to imagine a ball that would be better than the one he had made with his own hands. That ball was familiar, he was comfortable with it, and it was really hard for him to give it up. As beautiful and sturdy as the new ball might be, the old one still had an allure he couldn't quite shake. A lot of people feel about their lives the same way the boy felt about his ball, especially when they sense that God is calling them to something new. They like what's familiar, what's comfortable, and they're reluctant to leave it behind, even if they are reasonably certain

Children in Kenya play soccer with a ball made from a bundle of old plastic bags and string.

In Tanzania, Richard would love to play soccer using a real ball.

that to do so would be to follow God's leading. Hanging on to something that might be good, they miss what's even better.

To be honest, we were tempted to say no to God's call to World Vision. We loved our old life. But God was calling us to something new, and we just couldn't pass it up. We didn't want to be like Jonah who, in the belly of the fish, had an epiphany about the grace we forfeit when we refuse to follow God (Jonah 2:8). We didn't want to hang on to a ball of "trash" when we could have the real thing. What are you hanging on to that might be keeping you from obeying God's call?

—RENEÉ

ANSWERED PRAYERS

YOU ARE THE ANSWER TO SOMEONE'S PRAYER.

*"You did not choose me, but I chose you and appointed
you to go and bear fruit—fruit that will last. Then the
Father will give you whatever you ask in my name."*

JESUS IN JOHN 15:16

SO HOW DOES God answer our prayers? Have you ever wondered how
He processes the billions of prayers offered to Him each day? At times
God intervenes powerfully and directly in our lives. He unlocked the
doors to free Peter from prison, He saved Paul from a shipwreck, and even
today He still heals and rescues. But there is another way He answers
prayers, and that way is much more common and often overlooked.

Octaviana lived in the majestic Andes Mountains of Peru, at an alti-
tude of fourteen thousand feet on a hillside dotted with mud-brick huts
and populated by sheep, goats, and llamas. The natural beauty of that place
served as a tragically dissonant background for the suffering of this mother
of three young children. She had just been widowed, losing her husband to
a respiratory infection, possibly tuberculosis, for which he had received

Late in the evening, a farmer herds his llamas in Octaviana's village in Peru.

treatment too late. Now, alone on the mountain in the harsh climate of the high Andes, Octaviana had to find a way for her little family to survive. Plowing, planting, harvesting, and raising livestock, in addition to parenting three small children, was hard work without a husband. But she worked ... and she prayed.

Reneé and I sat in her crumbling hut and listened as she poured out her story with sadness and tears. At a loss for words, yet sensing that she was a woman of faith, I asked her specifically what she prayed for. Her answer changed my view of prayer forever: "I pray that God will not forget me and my children on this mountain. I pray that He will send help." Here, almost three miles high in the Andes, some six thousand miles from my home in Seattle, Octaviana had been praying for help— and God had sent me, the president of World Vision. God chose me as the answer to her prayer.

In Revelation 8 we get a glimpse of just what becomes of the prayers we offer to God: "Another angel, who had a golden censer, came and stood at

Bright clothes and majestic scenery belie the hard life for many rural families in the Andes Mountains of Peru.

the altar. He was given much incense to offer, with the prayers of all God's people, on the golden altar in front of the throne."

Our prayers come before the throne of God. And we are told in Ephesians that "we are [His] handiwork, created in Christ Jesus to do good works, which God prepared in advance for us to do" (Ephesians 2:10). Is it not possible, even likely, that God heard Octaviana's prayers and sent me—because I had been created in Christ Jesus to do this good work in her life, a good work prepared in advance for me to do?

Today, as you read this, millions of people around the world are praying: an orphan in India, a widow in Niger, a teenager in an inner city, an elderly woman in your neighborhood, someone struggling to raise a disabled child, another person just diagnosed with cancer. And they are crying out to God through prayer. Might you be the one God is sending? Might you be the answer to someone's prayer?

—RICH

THROUGH
FILTERED EYES

WE ARE GOD'S CHILDREN, DEARLY LOVED AND
VALUABLE BEYOND MEASURE.

*Now in Christ Jesus you who once were far away have
been brought near through the blood of Christ.*

EPHESIANS 2:13

"MOTHER BLINDNESS" is what my daughter, Grace, calls the condition that enables me to enthuse over the smallest of my children's and my grandson's accomplishments, to pronounce a simple art project a "masterpiece" or a piece of music, "breathtaking." If you're a parent, you know what I mean. In fact, you've probably experienced it too; you just didn't know this condition had a name. However, it was not until I met with Nagavani and her mother that I truly appreciated its significance.

Nagavani's small village outside of Vellore, India, is home to men and women, boys and girls, who are Dalits, members of the lowest caste in Indian society, forced to live alone in a remote location, cut off from the rest of the world. Despite her home's isolation, Nagavani had been swept up into the stream of commerce, sold into bonded labor so that the rest of her family could survive. For Nagavani, this meant that she would spend each day of

her young life filling little paper boxes—1,444 of them to be exact—with matches. When I asked her what the hardest part of being a bonded laborer had been, she told me that it was looking out the window of the matchbox factory while she was working each day, seeing other children walking to school. It reminded her that, because of who she was, an untouchable and a slave, she was, by any measure she could understand, worthless except for what her labor could produce each day for the factory owner.

But through the intervention of her community, Nagavani had been released from bondage; she was no longer a slave to the demands of the matchbox factory owner. Yet she and her family were still enslaved by their vision of themselves as social outcasts, insignificant and of little value. In fact, as I sat with Nagavani and a group of local women, her mother spoke up and asked, "Why are you here? What do you see when you look at us?"

Of course, I saw them simply as hardworking women, eager to provide for themselves and their families, very similar to women we had seen in other villages. Yet these women knew that when their neighbors looked at them, they could view them only through the filtered eyes of culture and custom.

I found myself thinking about the filter God uses when He looks at us. When He looks at the world He created, what does He see? He sees His children, dearly loved

THIS PAGE AND FACING PAGE: Young girls in India might be considered useless in some communities, but in God's eyes they are loved and valued beyond measure.

and valuable beyond measure, so valuable in fact that He willingly sacrificed His only Son. Once we through faith become part of God's family, when God looks at us, He sees Jesus. "Father blindness," you might say.

—Reneé

CONTENTMENT IS
AN ACQUIRED TASTE

WE FIND CONTENTMENT ONCE WE LEARN TO SEE EVERYTHING IN LIFE AS A GIFT OR OPPORTUNITY. PERSPECTIVE IS EVERYTHING. HAPPINESS IS A CHOICE.

I know what it is to be in need, and I know what it is to have plenty. I have learned the secret of being content in any and every situation, whether well fed or hungry, whether living in plenty or in want. I can do all this through him who gives me strength.

PHILIPPIANS 4:12–13

ONE OF THE QUINTESSENTIAL DECLARATIONS my wife spouted to our five children with great regularity was this: "Happiness is a choice—make it!" This was typically uttered when one of the kids was moping over some deprivation—the newest video game or the cutest-ever dress—or perhaps disappointment over that day's dinner menu. "This is not a restaurant" was another of her frequent exhortations. But we grown-ups aren't all that different from our kids. Contentment does not come naturally to most of us; it is definitely an acquired taste.

Finedia and Maggie huddled in their rain-soaked hut when Rich first met them in Zambia.

Four years later, Maggie's eyes and smile reflect the transformation in her life.

Finedia was seventy-two and caring for her seven-year-old great-granddaughter, Maggie, when I met her in Zambia. Perhaps more than any person I had ever met, Finedia had learned to be content in the midst of want. Why was this old woman caring for a child? Because everyone else—two generations of Finedia's family—had died. Elderly, homeless, hungry, and grieving, Finedia and her little Maggie soldiered on. They lived in an abandoned hut, and Finedia worked all day, when she could, for just a cup of cornmeal. I think what struck me most about Finedia was that she simply accepted her lot; she did the best she could, without any sense of entitlement.

It has been said that Jesus plus nothing equals everything, and that is true. If you have Jesus, you are a child of the King. You have been rescued from darkness and promised eternal life. He loves you beyond your imagining, and He died that you might live. Offer Jesus your half-full glass, and He will fill it to overflowing. No matter what your hardships, you are still His child, because the reverse is also true: Jesus minus everything is still everything. If you have Jesus, anything else you possess is a bonus.

Four years after I first met Finedia, I returned. Thanks to World Vision she now had food to eat, a modest house, and a couple of chairs to sit in. And of course she had Maggie, now a beautiful twelve-year-old and the joy of Finedia's life. At seventy-six, Finedia had found contentment in the midst of want. It is elusive, but we can find it too if we learn to see our lives through the lens of God's abundance.

Helen Keller, born both blind and deaf, claimed this truth: "So much has been given to me I have not time to ponder over that which has been denied." Jesus asks us to find our contentment in Him alone. But it is still an acquired taste. Happiness is a choice. Finedia's choice. Your choice. And mine.

—RICH

WASHING DISHES

*If the willingness is there, the gift is acceptable according
to what one has, not according to what he does not have.*

2 CORINTHIANS 8:12

A QUICK INTERNET SEARCH REVEALS multiple suggestions for the best way to wash dishes. You can, for instance, find four, nineteen, or twenty-four steps to a clean dish as well as some YouTube videos for visual learners. I've washed my share of dishes, but honestly, I've never been that interested in the science of dishwashing, nor do I think that washing dishes is actually so difficult that it requires research.

Then again, I might be wrong. A visit with Editor, the mother of six children living in a rural community in Zambia, made me think I might need to reconsider. She'd been working with World Vision staff to improve her family's health. Together, they drilled a borehole to provide clean water and pit latrines to improve sanitation, and Editor was able to secure a loan to buy a cow. So I was surprised by her answer when I asked about the most important thing she had learned since World Vision came to her village. She told me she had learned to construct a dish rack. A dish rack? It seems that a dish rack on stilts was just what she needed to keep

In rural Kenya, simple things like a dish rack can transform a woman's life.

her clean dishes off the ground and away from her pig's curious tongue.

Rich often says that tackling poverty is rocket science, and he's right. Addressing its root causes is not an amateur activity. Identifying and then solving the problems faced by those in need can be complicated. But sometimes—as in Editor's case—making a difference is as simple as a clean dish.

A woman's day begins at sunrise in Kenya.

In the face of the world's overwhelming problems, I'm often tempted to believe I have little to offer. I'm certainly no expert in hydrology or agronomy, but given the extent of my experience, I might be an expert in dishwashing. And apparently in God's economy, that's important too!

British philosopher Edmund Burke once said, "Nobody made a greater mistake than he who did nothing because he could do only a little." I can't solve the problems of the world, but I can do something, just like the woman in Luke 21. Jesus and His disciples sat watching as people brought their offerings to the temple treasury. Seeing a woman drop two very small copper coins into the box, Jesus said, "This poor widow has put in more than all the others. All these people gave their gifts out of their wealth; but she out of her poverty put in all she had to live on" (Luke 21:3–4).

Imagine if He could say the same of us, if for Jesus' sake we put it all in, certain that He can use what little we have to offer to make a difference in the world. There's a Franciscan benediction that says: May God bless you with enough foolishness to believe that you really can make a difference in this world, so that you are able, with God's grace, to do what others claim cannot be done.

So do something foolish. Go out and wash some dishes!

—RENEÉ

SPIRITUAL BODY BUILDERS

WITH OUR GREAT SPIRITUAL WEALTH COMES THE RESPONSIBILITY
TO PUT WHAT WE HAVE LEARNED INTO PRACTICE.

*When the king heard the words of the Book of the Law, he
tore his robes. . . . "Great is the LORD's anger that burns
against us because those who have gone before us have
not obeyed the words of this book; they have not acted in
accordance with all that is written there concerning us."*

2 KINGS 22:11,13

DID YOU KNOW THAT THERE ARE roughly 340,000 churches in
America? In case you're not good with big numbers, let me say it this way:
for every Starbucks in America, there are about twenty-eight churches!
In fact, there are even twice as many churches as there are gas stations.
Access to the Christian faith and teaching from Scripture is available to
anyone in America who wants it.

Not so in the former Soviet Republic of Georgia. People in the village
of Uraveli hadn't had a church for four hundred years. Under communis-
tic rule every effort was made to stamp out Christianity, but the people still

After years of communism and suppressed Christianity in Albania, faith is being reborn in eight-year-old Andrea Laska's community.

hungered for God. So when World Vision offered Sunday school programs for the children, we were welcomed with gladness.

Gulo, a sixty-three-year-old math teacher, said, "I was reading the Bible even during the Soviet period. I was hiding it. Now I am so happy to talk to a new generation about Christianity." Gulo was so motivated that she organized the community, raised contributions, and mobilized volunteers to build a church. "Finally we made it. We now have a place where we can go and pray." Today the church is full on Sundays, and so are the children's Sunday school classes. Uraveli is being transformed by God's Word.

In the book of 2 Kings, we learn that the Scriptures had been lost for generations until one day the high priest found a copy of the law of Moses while they were renovating the temple. When the book was taken to Judah's King Josiah, he read what the Scriptures said and was so upset that he *tore his robes*. The Scriptures had convicted him of just how far the nation had drifted away from God's truth, so Josiah

Adults in Armenia are now free to share their faith with children.

responded. He gathered all of the people and their leaders at the temple, read aloud from the Book of the Law, and publicly committed "to follow the LORD and keep his commands, statutes and decrees with all his heart and all his soul" (2 Kings 23:3). Then King Josiah went on a campaign to reform the nation and bring it into alignment with God's Word.

So what about us? My son, Pete, is a junior high youth pastor near Chicago. He once preached a message to his kids about what he called "spiritual body builders." Pete's observation was that body builders dedicate their whole lives to building huge muscles, but their muscles are just for show. They don't use them for anything worthwhile; they just strut around and show them off. And when we go to church, read our Bibles, have our quiet times, and go to Christian conferences, we too can build some impressive spiritual muscles, but unless we use those spiritual muscles to change our lives, build the church, love our neighbors, and care for the sick and the poor, we, too, are just posers. Let us not take God's truth for granted. Like Josiah, should we not "tear our robes" and change our lives?

—RICH

CHANGED FROM
THE INSIDE OUT

CLOTHE YOURSELF WITH CHRIST.

*As God's chosen people, holy and dearly loved, clothe
yourselves with compassion, kindness, humility, gentleness
and patience. Bear with each other and forgive whatever
grievances you may have against one another. Forgive as
the Lord forgave you. And over all these virtues put on love.*

COLOSSIANS 3:12–14

Dear Reneé,

We the child mothers learning tailoring in the centre
are pleased to have you in our centre. We give you an
African dress we have made as a gift in rememberance.

May God bless you.

I CARRY THIS LITTLE NOTE around in my Bible to remind me of the very special group of young women I met at the Children of War Center in Gulu, Northern Uganda. The note originally accompanied a beautiful batik garment, handmade for me by these dear sisters from the Child-Mother's Group at the center, all survivors of a bloody war waged by Joseph Kony and the Lord's Resistance Army (LRA). They had been abducted, taken from their homes to serve as sex slaves for army commanders, and each of them had given birth while being held captive. But having escaped Kony's clutches, they found their way to the Children of War Center. There, the staff showered them with the love of Jesus, and they received counseling, medical care, and vocational training. My new dress was a product of one of their lessons.

As I slipped the dress over my head, they smiled, proud of their work and proud, no doubt, of how far they had come since escaping the LRA. In just a few short months at the Center, they had gone from slavery to freedom, from shame and degradation to the pride of accomplishment, from being

For these young mothers in Zambia, sewing classes bring opportunity and hope.

Girls in Uganda, survivors of a bloody war waged by Joseph Kony and the LRA, dance as part of their therapy at the Children's War Center.

outcasts to being members of a family. Although I put on the beautiful dress, it was they who had been transformed.

Just as in this Child-Mothers Group, true transformation comes about when we are changed not merely on the outside, but inwardly as well. While the Bible uses the illustration of clothing to talk about the process whereby followers of Jesus Christ are made into His likeness, that transformation is much more than an external makeover, much more than the taking off of one garment and the putting on of another. Yet that is the image Paul used: "You were taught, with regard to your former way of life, to put off your old self, which is being corrupted by its deceitful desires; to be made new in the attitude of your minds; and to put on the new self, created to be like God in true righteousness and holiness" (Ephesians 4:22–24).

As God's chosen people, holy and dearly loved, we are to be clothed with the virtues that characterize the life of Jesus. We are to be His ambassadors, transformed by His grace and living in such a way that others can see the Savior through us (2 Corinthians 5:20). Although the beautiful dress given me at the Children of War Center changed the way I looked on the outside, more beautiful still are the changes that Jesus wants to bring about in my life by the power of His Holy Spirit on the inside.

—Reneé

ONE STONE AT A TIME

*We kept at it, repairing and rebuilding the wall. The whole
wall was soon joined together and halfway to its intended
height because the people had a heart for the work.*

NEHEMIAH 4:6 MSG

NEHEMIAH FOUND THE STATUS QUO UNACCEPTABLE.
Decades after the Babylonians had destroyed the Holy City, the great
wall surrounding Jerusalem still lay in ruins. To Nehemiah this was a
disgrace in the eyes of God and it saddened him. "When I heard these things,
I sat down and wept. For some days I mourned and fasted and prayed before
the God of heaven" (Nehemiah 1:4). Then this one man embraced a vision
to do the impossible: he would lead the Jews in rebuilding the great wall and
give honor to God by restoring this symbol of God's greatness.

As the president of World Vision, I can relate to large and daunting
problems like the one Nehemiah faced. Two billion people in the world
live in desperate poverty, and nearly twenty thousand children under
the age of five needlessly die every day. Trying to "save the world" can be

A young child in India clings to his mother after a disaster took their home and possessions.

overwhelming and discouraging. But God gave me a different perspective on this through a six-year-old boy named Vikas.

It was the last day of a trip to India, just after the Gujarat earthquake, in the very last village I visited. As we were driving away, a desperate and pleading mother ran up to the window of my car. The driver kept going, but I had just enough time to see her holding a little boy with no feet—and then they were gone. That image burned itself into my mind, and when I returned home, I couldn't get it out of my head. I had been trying to facilitate help for the thousands who had been affected by the earthquake, but the Lord seemed to be showing me this one little boy.

A few e-mails and a few weeks later, World Vision India located Vikas. I learned that his legs had been crushed in the earthquake, and it would cost about $300 for surgery and prosthetic limbs. I felt convicted that I should pay for this because I knew that seeing Vikas was no accident—clearly, God had shown this little guy to me. And even though tens of thousands of victims needed help, I knew they would all have to be helped one at a time.

Nehemiah understood that great walls are repaired just one stone at a time, so he organized the people to each do their part: "Above the Horse Gate, the priests made repairs, each in front of his own house" (Nehemiah 3:28). The impossible task of rebuilding the wall of Jerusalem was completed in fifty-two days because each person tackled the section of the wall that lay right in front of them.

A few months later, I received an e-mail from India with a photograph of little Vikas smiling and standing on his brand-new legs. Oswald Chambers once wrote: "The great hindrance in spiritual life is that we will look for big things to do. Jesus took a towel . . . and began to wash the disciples' feet."

God's heart is broken today over the ruins of poverty, injustice, and suffering in this world. Do you weep for those who suffer just as Nehemiah wept for Jerusalem? Don't stop there. Act! What section of the wall has God placed in front of you?

—Rich

RECLAMATION PROJECT

WE SERVE A GOD OF SECOND CHANCES.

"The Son of Man came to seek and to save what was lost."

JESUS IN LUKE 19:10

THE FIVE LITTLE GIRLS GIGGLED with delight as they watched my unsuccessful efforts to do what they could do with ease. It turned out that molding a piece of clay into anything remotely resembling a griddle on which to fry tortillas was deceptively difficult. Nonetheless, I stepped forward to try my hand at making a *comale*. I had watched Sarah and her daughters making them and thought, *How challenging can this be?* The answer? Very challenging indeed!

Sarah's family had been hard-hit by Hurricane Mitch. Their biggest loss was the tin roof of their mud-brick home, which had blown away during the worst of the storm. Now they needed to start over but didn't have funds to begin. Sarah had heard about Aguadessa, the World Vision microfinance lending institution in Guatemala, and she decided to approach it for a small loan to begin a business making *comales*.

For most people living on the edge of poverty, acquiring capital is nearly impossible. Without collateral or a track record of business success, most

A woman in Mexico fries tortillas on a *comale*.

banks won't make a small, individual loan, and local lenders often gouge poor clients with high interest rates. But through microfinance lending organizations, men and women with an entrepreneurial spirit and a willingness to work hard can join together to borrow the small amount (usually between fifty and five hundred dollars) they need to start a business and turn their lives around.

A little water, flour, and a small loan make for a new start.

Zacchaeus, the chief tax collector in the city of Jericho, needed to turn his life around too. On the day Jesus was passing through, Zacchaeus climbed into a sycamore tree so he could catch a glimpse of the preacher who, just outside the city, had given sight to a man born blind. Imagine his surprise when Jesus, looking up into the tree, called Zacchaeus down and then invited Himself to dinner (Luke 19).

Surely aware that this act would bring the crowd's disapproval, Jesus nevertheless sought out this corrupt tax collector. Where others saw a cheat and a traitor, Jesus saw a reclamation project. Others may have given up on Zacchaeus, but Jesus did not. He took the initiative, and Zacchaeus responded by embracing the opportunity Jesus gave him to change his life.

All that some people need to turn their lives around is an opportunity. Zacchaeus was one of those people, and so is Sarah. As the result of a loan in an amount most would consider insignificant, her life has changed forever. She's now an entrepreneur. With her success making *comales* and selling them in the local market, she's been able to replace the roof on her house, and her daughters are in school. Sarah simply needed a chance to begin again.

We serve a God of second chances. He gave one to Zacchaeus. He gave one to Sarah. Do you need one? Just ask.

—Reneé

THE FRAGRANCE OF CHRIST

WHEN WE PUT GOD FIRST IN OUR LIVES, WE BRING THE AROMA OF HOPE TO THOSE AROUND US.

For we are to God the pleasing aroma of Christ among those who are being saved and those who are perishing. To the one we are an aroma that brings death; to the other, an aroma that brings life. And who is equal to such a task? Unlike so many, we do not peddle the word of God for profit. On the contrary, in Christ we speak before God with sincerity, as those sent from God.

2 CORINTHIANS 2:15–17

WHAT AROMA DO PEOPLE AROUND YOU NOTICE?

After several days on a medical boat on Brazil's Rio Negro river, I'm afraid my own aroma wasn't so pleasing, but the trip had been magical. This broad and mighty river that eventually joins the Amazon is home to a dazzling array of plants, animals, and people. But many of those people are poor and extremely vulnerable, which is why World Vision partnered with a Brazilian church and operated a medical boat to provide basic care for those who live along the river.

A floating health center dispenses medical, dental and spiritual care to people living along the Rio Negro river in Brazil.

During our trip I was reading *Light in the Jungle* by Leo Halliwell, a book written in 1959 that chronicles the lives of a missionary couple who traveled up and down the Amazon River for three decades on their own medical boat. Here is their poignant description of the people living along the rivers:

> *"They were a people who needed help in a hundred ways: people starving in the midst of plenty; ravaged by disease in the midst of this humid lushness; people who hungered not for food so much as for a vision, for a reason to live, for purpose and goal and direction."*

More than forty years later, many of the same needs—both medical and spiritual—still existed. Enter Joel, the dentist. He had quit his lucrative dental practice so he could serve on the medical boat full-time. Joel is perhaps the most joyful Christian I have ever met. Every morning, after sleeping in his hammock on the open deck, he led the music for our devotions, playing hymns and praise music on his guitar and singing with great abandon.

Joel, a dentist who gave up a lucrative practice to work on the boat, plays the tambourine and sings with infectious abandon.

One day I watched Joel as he ministered to children sitting in his dental chair. He spent a minute getting to know the children and putting them at ease. He always asked them if they had a best friend and then explained that Jesus was his best Friend. If they didn't seem to know about Jesus, Joel reached for a kind of Rubik's Cube device with pictures on its sides and used it to plainly present the gospel. Finally, Joel prayed with each of the children, fixed their teeth, and sent them off with a new smile that went beyond simply their improved dental condition.

My most enduring image of this exuberant man came when he hoisted above his head a very large fish he had caught. For half an hour or so, he posed on both decks, laughing and celebrating his prize catch. No one Joel encountered could miss the "aroma of Christ." Such was the joyful spirit of this man who truly was a fisher of men.

When we make God more important than everything else in our life—above money, comfort, career, self-interest—we begin to love what He loves and treasure what He treasures. That's when people notice His fragrance in us.

—RICH

WHAT'S MINE TO DO?

FIND OUT WHAT GOD IS CALLING YOU TO DO—AND DO IT!

I can do everything through him who
gives me strength.

PHILIPPIANS 4:13

ONE OF MY HUSBAND'S guilty pleasures is watching *America's Got Talent*, the reality television series where amateur entertainers compete for a million dollars. So imagine our surprise as we sat in the living room drinking tea with our Palestinian hostess and noticed that playing quietly on the television in the corner was *Arabs Got Talent,* the Middle Eastern equivalent of *AGT*!

We were staying overnight in Aboud, a small Christian village in the West Bank, where centuries-old olive groves had been uprooted by Israeli forces so that they could build a security wall. The community had purchased some new olive trees, but they stood in white plastic buckets rather than in the ground, presumably so they could be moved if necessary. Earlier in the day, I had hiked among the buckets with Rawah, who was looking forward to leaving Aboud to attend Birzeit University. "But what is the use?" one

The Dome of the Rock shines in the Jerusalem sun.

villager asked me. "Our children have no future. They go to university and then return home prepared to do jobs that don't exist. They become tour guides instead of world leaders."

When evening came, we slept at the home of Hiam, a nurse educated in the United States and England. Before her retirement, road closures caused by the security wall had kept her from traveling to the medical clinic in Ramala, and she was forced to commute to her office over the hillsides riding on a donkey. Her nephew, with his wife and little girl, joined us as we sat watching *Arabs Got Talent*, and he shared his concerns about the safety of his young family in this community.

When I'm confronted with a situation like this—one that's too big for me to handle—or when I'm frustrated by the sheer injustice of something happening right in front of me, I often tell myself, "This (whatever the problem might be) is not mine to fix." It's what a friend once said to me when I was fussing about something that was, frankly, none of my business. And while it does help to remind me that I'm not always responsible for making everything right, I find I sometimes use it as an excuse to do nothing.

More helpful is the question Lynne Hybels taught me to ask: "What's mine to do?" Lynne, a longtime advocate for peace and justice in the Holy Land, had accompanied us on this trip and understood my sense of frustration: *How can I help? What can I do to make a difference in these people's lives? Maybe there really is nothing I can do. Maybe it's best if I just go home and stick to my knitting.*

Do you ever feel that way? Are the problems confronting the world or your community or even your family just too big to get your mind around, let alone try to fix? Don't give in to the temptation to do nothing because you can't do everything. God is not calling you to fix every problem, but more likely than not, He is calling you to do something. Find out what that something is and then do it with all your heart.

—RENÉE

Schoolgirls make their way past sheep in Gaza.

WHY ME?

*Who shall separate us from the love of Christ? Shall
trouble or hardship or persecution or famine or
nakedness or danger or sword? . . . No, in all these things
we are more than conquerors through him who loved us.*

ROMANS 8:35, 37

WHO OF US HAS NOT ASKED, "WHY ME?"

That very thought flashed through my mind when my own dear wife, Reneé, was diagnosed with cancer. Embedded somewhere deeply in our Christian consciousness is the sense that bad things shouldn't happen to good people. But in Romans 8, Paul taught exactly the opposite: he clearly stated that hardship, famine, persecution, and danger *will* most certainly prey upon believers. Yet Paul's comfort to us in light of that harsh reality is the life-giving reality that nothing can separate us from the love of Christ. In fact, experience has shown me that people living in poverty understand this truth more completely than those of us living in comfort.

Reneé and I met such a woman at an unlikely church service in Haiti less than a year after the terrible earthquake. Just outside Port-au-Prince a city of crude tents sprawled as far as the eye could see. Perhaps ten thousand homeless lived on that barren patch of dust and dirt.

It was Sunday, and hundreds of people were making their way through the maze of tents. Dressed in their best white shirts and blouses, they were converging on a larger tent structure—a makeshift church pieced together with scrap lumber, corrugated tin, and tarps—topped with a rugged cross. That morning Reneé and I learned a transformative lesson about the power of faith. For more than two hours, this church of hurting refugees poured out their praise—and their pain—to the One who, despite what circumstances may have suggested, still loved them.

A strong and dignified woman led the choir, and we were struck by her demeanor, her passion for Jesus, and her fervent praise. But she stood on just one leg and clapped with only one arm.

A devastating earthquake hit Haiti on January 12, 2010, killing at least 220,000 people and affecting three million.

Demosi had lost both an arm and a leg on the day of the earthquake. But there she was, leading the choir and praising her Lord enthusiastically.

Meeting with Demosi afterward in her little tent, we sensed we were in the presence of one of God's great servants. Demosi wasn't asking God, "Why me?" Instead of bitterness, Demosi had gratitude toward God because He had spared her life that day. He had given her not only a second chance

Though Demosi (red head scarf) lost two limbs in the earthquake, she still praises God each day.

to raise her girls but also the opportunity to be a source of strength for her community and to serve her Lord. When Reneé asked what she would like us to tell people about her, Demosi smiled broadly and said, "Tell them that Lazarus is alive again!" Tradition says that after Jesus raised Lazarus from the dead, he became a powerful missionary on the island of Cyprus.

It has now been ten years since Reneé's breast cancer diagnosis, and I remember vividly her remarkable attitude as she walked through it. "Why *not* me?" she used to say. "I have a family that loves me and a strong faith in the Lord. Better me than someone who doesn't have those things." Like Demosi, Reneé had claimed God's promise that she could be "more than [a conqueror]" through the strength of Christ's unwavering love (Romans 8:37).

—RICH

A NEW NAME

WE FIND OUR TRUE IDENTITY IN CHRIST.

"Fear not, for I have redeemed you; I have summoned you by name; you are mine."

ISAIAH 43:1

ALTHOUGH HE WAS THE MOST INTELLIGENT of Dorothy's companions, what the Scarecrow wanted most was a brain. The Cowardly Lion wanted courage, but he was already the bravest among them. And the Tin Man? He wanted a heart, even though the heart he had overflowed with compassion for others. It took the efforts of a "wizard" to help each character in *The Wizard of Oz* discover that the very thing they most longed for was already within them. Like Dorothy's friends, we also have within us the capacity to be more than we may think we are.

How does who you think you are compare with the person God created you to be? Second Corinthians 5:17 says that, "If anyone is in Christ, he is a new creation; the old has gone, the new has come!" When we enter into a relationship with Jesus Christ as our Lord and Savior, the old labels no longer apply. We have a new identity, a new name! We are children of the King, beloved, forgiven, redeemed. We are a new creation and we need to start acting as if God's name for us was really true, because it is!

In the midst of a tent camp, Demosi receives medical care from physical therapist Jony St. Louis.

Names are important. They help to give us our sense of identity. In the Bible, names often reflect the circumstances of one's birth or a parent's expectations. But we see in the Bible that God also changed some people's names. He changed *Abram* to *Abraham* as a sign of His promise that Abraham would be the father of many nations. *Simon* became

Sprawling tent camps sprang up in Haiti after the 2010 earthquake, transforming the landscape of the capital city, Port-au-Prince.

Peter, and *Saul* became *Paul* to mark the transformation God was to bring about in their characters and usefulness to Him.

Demosi is a modern-day example of someone whose name was changed because of a transformation God brought about in her life. Once a shopkeeper on the roadside in Port-au-Prince, Haiti, Demosi is now a double amputee as a result of injuries sustained in the 2010 earthquake. But that's not who she is; that's not her true identity. Rather, she told me confidently, she is Lazarus come back from the dead. Latent within this quiet, unassuming woman was a pillar of strength, a person of remarkable resilience and courage in the face of overwhelming odds. She would never have thought of herself as a role model for others, yet God has transformed her into an encourager for the thousands of others in her community who have also experienced loss.

Just as He did in Demosi's life, God longs to bring out in each of us all He created us to be—not what we think we are, limited by our own self-images and imaginations, but what God says we are. He calls each of us by name and tells us that we are His very own. We are God's workmanship; we are more than conquerors. Let us begin today to live lives worthy of our God-given, purpose-filled name!

—RENEÉ

YIELDING TO THE POTTER'S HANDS

God uses adversity in our lives to deepen our faith and make us pleasing to Him.

> *This is the word that came to Jeremiah from the*
> *Lord: "Go down to the potter's house, and there I will*
> *give you my message." So I went down to the potter's*
> *house, and I saw him working at the wheel. But the*
> *pot he was shaping from the clay was marred in*
> *his hands; so the potter formed it into another pot,*
> *shaping it as seemed best to him.*
>
> ### Jeremiah 18:1–4

I ONCE SERVED AS CEO OF LENOX, America's fine china company, best known, since Woodrow Wilson was president, for crafting the White House china. As America's premier potter, so to speak, I learned a thing or two about how mere earth and clay are transformed into something both beautiful and useful.

The potter must first form the clay under great pressure into a pleasing shape. This raw, pressed clay must then go into the kiln and be fired for many hours at temperatures in excess of two thousand degrees. The pieces that survive the ordeal without cracking are then carefully coated with a glaze of liquid glass and then sent again into the brutal heat of the kiln, emerging this time with the lovely gloss that characterizes the most beautiful china. But the process is still not complete. The potter must then bring the piece to life by painting it with vibrant colors and designs and then painstakingly embellishing it with brilliant 24k gold. Then back it goes into the kiln for yet more heat and fire. Only then is the final work of art ready for service. Fine china is made beautiful by the pressure and the heat that burn out its imperfections and allow its beauty to shine. And not all vessels will make the grade. Clay that is too brittle—too unwilling to be shaped—and clay that is too pliable—too amorphous to hold a shape—will not survive the crucible.

Jony and Demosi are both moving forward on the road to recovery.

Children in Haiti suffered much loss and trauma following the devastating earthquake. But slowly, life returns.

Jony St. Louis knows something about pressure and heat. On the day of the Haiti earthquake, he lost his wife and his home. He was torn by grief and almost inconsolable, but he soon found consolation in coming alongside and consoling others. So many people who had lost limbs in the earthquake needed rehabilitation, therapy, and prosthetic limbs, and Jony—a trained physical therapist—could help. He threw himself into his work, burning out the pain from his own soul by easing the pain of others. Demosi, the inspirational woman in the previous story who had lost both her arm and her leg in the quake, was one of Jony's first patients. Jony walked with Demosi, encouraging her through her darkest hours. In His mysterious ways, God was using Jony to lift up Demosi, and Demosi provided the inspiration Jony needed to carry on. Pressure and heat produced something of beauty in both.

As God shapes and molds our life and our character, we, too, will face pressure and heat. We, too, will go from the Potter's determined hands into the fire and back out again. We will suffer losses and disappointments, setbacks and obstacles, pressure and heat. We don't usually ask for these things, and we don't usually welcome them when they come, but this is how God shapes us into people who are both pleasing and useful to Him, people He can then use to demonstrate His love and reveal His character to a watching world.

—RICH

ALCHEMY: THE SCIENCE OF TURNING TIN INTO GOLD

GOD CAN TAKE THE ORDINARY AND TRANSFORM IT INTO SOMETHING EXTRAORDINARY FOR HIM.

Brothers, think of what you were when you were called. Not many of you were wise by human standards; not many were influential; not many were of noble birth. But God chose the foolish things of the world to shame the wise; God chose the weak things of the world to shame the strong. He chose the lowly things of this world and the despised things—and the things that are not—to nullify the things that are, so that no one many boast before him. It is because of him that you are in Christ Jesus, who has become for us wisdom from God—that is, our righteousness, holiness and redemption. Therefore, as it is written: "Let him who boasts boast in the Lord."

I CORINTHIANS 1:26–31

IN A SIDE-BY-SIDE COMPARISON, I don't think anyone would mistake me for Hillary Clinton, but in a small village in Northern Uganda, I can see why someone might be confused. Rich, our daughter Hannah, and I were visiting the village where Faith Esther, my daughter's sponsored child, lives. As is often the case when Rich travels to World Vision projects, people were singing and dancing in celebration of his arrival. But this party was over the top. Clearly, this wasn't just a spontaneous gathering of people wanting to greet the president of World Vision US. A huge ceremony was underway. We got more nervous when we noticed the gifts piled beside our chairs, so Rich sent someone to find out what was going on. Imagine our surprise when he returned with news that the villagers were under the impression that we were the former president Bill Clinton

Just as a simple piece of rope can be transformed into a child's swing, God can make us into something beautiful and useful to Him.

and his wife Hillary, accompanied by our daughter, Chelsea! When the village chief was told that the president of World Vision US was planning a visit, he focused on the words *president* and *US* and concluded that Bill, Hillary, and Chelsea were dropping by.

Now we had a decision to make. Should we play along so as not to disappoint this appreciative crowd of well-meaning people, or should we tell them we were not who they thought we were? After a few minutes of deliberation, we concluded that it was only right to tell them we were not the Clintons. As the saying goes, you can't make a silk purse out of a sow's ear, and you can't turn the Stearns family into the First Family. You can't transform something ordinary into something extraordinary. Or can you?

In times past, alchemists tried to do exactly that. They sought a method for turning base metals like tin into gold, a way of making

Water in the desert country of Niger is valued like gold—and so is a chance to swim at the end of a hot day.

something of little value into something precious. They failed, of course, but God never fails. He takes the lowly things of this world—the foolish, the weak, and the despised—and makes them into something beautiful and useful for Him.

In a world that places a high value on appearance, ability, accomplishment, and acquisition, we can find it difficult to believe that God can use us to accomplish His purposes here on earth. We too easily take our cues from a culture that assigns value to people based upon title, appearance, résumé, or bank account rather than our willingness to be available to God. But what the alchemists of old tried in vain to accomplish, God can do in the lives of ordinary people like us, not because we are worthy, but because He is able. By His saving grace, He can turn ashes into a crown of beauty, replace mourning with gladness, exchange despair for a garment of praise. He can even turn a sow's ear into a silk purse or tin into gold.

—RENEÉ

A DROP IN THE BUCKET

HELPING SOMEONE ELSE IS NEVER INSIGNIFICANT.

"Whoever welcomes one of these little children in my name welcomes me; and whoever welcomes me does not welcome me but the one who sent me."

JESUS IN MARK 9:37

GLOBAL POVERTY STATISTICS can be overwhelming, even to those of us at World Vision who have dedicated our lives to helping. More than two billion people live on less than $2 a day. More than 1 billion don't have clean water to drink; hundreds of millions are chronically hungry and malnourished. And children suffer the most. Every four seconds a child under the age of five dies simply because he is poor and doesn't have his basic needs met.

In light of these staggering statistics, I am often asked, "Isn't my small contribution just a tiny drop in a very large bucket?" The answer depends on how you see the world.

A few years back I was traveling in Myanmar with some World Vision supporters. Our local staff had arranged for kids from our street children program to perform songs and native dances for us. It was a marvelous

A young boy in Myanmar carries his malnourished brother to a World Vision feeding center.

evening as we witnessed how these homeless children's lives had been transformed and how they had been taught to perform at a level equal to any American school children. At the show's finale, a little boy in a wheelchair, cobbled together from spare bicycle parts, was pushed onto the stage. He literally stole the show as, surrounded by the other children, he proceeded to sing in a voice so hauntingly beautiful it didn't seem possible that it was coming from his tiny, crippled body. There was not a dry eye in the audience.

His name was Htun Htun (pronounced Tun Tun) Win. He had been born with a deformed spine that caused open abscesses, paralysis, and a host of other problems. His inability to walk, except by pulling himself along on his hands, plus his incontinence, infections, and the resulting odor, were too much for his family, so they abandoned him to the streets. Htun Htun was just seven years old—and living at the train station and begging for money—when some of the other "street kids" from the World Vision program found him and brought him in to be helped.

Two spinal surgeries and two years later, Htun Htun no longer had abscesses on his spine. He had gained control of his bowels and was able to move his legs. He lived with his new friends at the World Vision home for street children. And he sang like a songbird because he now had something to sing about. This "throwaway" child was not a lost cause—not merely a statistic—he was precious in God's sight.

So, is helping one child just a small drop in a very large bucket? It's all a matter of perspective. Those who helped Htun Htun were not just putting their very small drop in the very large bucket of human suffering. No, they were filling Htun Htun's very small bucket to overflowing. If we see the world's needy children as millions of tiny buckets just waiting to be filled, the question changes to "How many buckets, Lord, do You want me to fill?"

—RICH

JESUS LOVES THE
LITTLE CHILDREN

NOTHING IS TOO HARD FOR GOD.

Ah, Sovereign LORD, you have made the heavens and
the earth by your great power and outstretched arm.
Nothing is too hard for you.

JEREMIAH 32:17

I LIKE HOW THE BIBLE DOESN'T SUGARCOAT THE FACTS. God's Word clearly shows that times of serious doubt often follow fast on the heels of great acts of faith. Think of Elijah who, after defeating the prophets of Baal, fled in fear from Queen Jezebel; or Peter who, after stepping out of the boat, began to sink beneath the waves. Then there was Jeremiah who, after obeying God's command to purchase a piece of land behind enemy lines, started to question God.

It all began when God alerted the imprisoned Jeremiah that his cousin was coming to persuade him to buy the property on which the Babylonian army was encamped. Convinced that this was God's will, Jeremiah readily agreed to buy it. But then doubts began to creep in.

"Does this make sense, Lord? We're in the middle of a war. Is this really a good time to invest in real estate?" Like Peter when the Lord beckoned

Sisters Sreychea, four, and Srey Poeu, three, beg all day and sleep all night on the streets of Phnom Penh, Cambodia.

him to walk on the water, Jeremiah began to look around, and he could not reconcile what he saw with what he knew.

We all go through times like that, times when our faith is shaken because of the circumstances around us:

> *Lord, I took this new job thinking it was what You wanted. Why isn't it working out?*
>
> *Lord, I was certain this was the man You wanted me to marry. Why does he want a divorce?*
>
> *Lord, You said You love children. Why are so many of them suffering?*

That's how I felt as I stood in the midst of hundreds of little Chinese girls who'd been abandoned by their parents because they weren't born male. From childhood, we are taught that Jesus loves the little children. But as I stood in a Chinese orphanage with so many discarded, thrown away children, I struggled to make sense of what I saw.

Then I remembered Jeremiah. From his perspective, Jeremiah couldn't imagine what a real estate deal had to do with the redemption of Israel. But rather than despair, in his confusion he prayed, reminding himself of God's nature and character: "Ah, Sovereign Lord, you have made the heavens and the earth by your great power and outstretched arm. Nothing is too hard for you" (Jeremiah 32:17).

Nothing. It is not too hard for God to rescue His people in the midst of war. And it's not too hard for God to end the suffering of little children. It's just that, perhaps, He's chosen us to help. In the same way that God entrusted Jeremiah to carry His message to Israel, He's also entrusted us to feed the hungry, clothe the naked, heal the sick, and care for the widows and orphans in their distress.

Not feeling up to the task? Having trouble reconciling what you see in your life with what you know to be true about God? Remember Jeremiah. That's right; nothing is too hard for the Lord.

—RENEÉ

HEROES OF
THE FAITH

I do not have time to tell about Gideon, Barak, Samson and
Jephthah, about David and Samuel and the prophets, who
through faith conquered kingdoms, administered justice,
and gained what was promised; who shut the mouths of
lions, quenched the fury of the flames, and escaped the edge
of the sword; whose weakness was turned to strength; and
who became powerful in battle and routed foreign armies.

HEBREWS 11:32–34

THE TSUNAMI HIT WITHOUT WARNING. In less than thirty minutes, tens of thousands of people died, and hundreds of miles of coastal villages were washed away. Just fifty yards from the sea in Batticaloa, Sri Lanka, the roof had been torn off a three-story building, indicating a wave at least forty feet high. I could see into a room on the third floor of this abandoned shell of a building. It was obviously the room of a teenage girl who had covered her walls with magazine covers and posters of pop stars. I don't know if she survived.

World Vision's Regional Operations Director Clarence Sutharsan was at home with his family that Sunday morning, far enough from the ocean to be safe. His phone rang, and he heard the frightened voice of the wife of one of his managers saying that the water had overwhelmed their home and they needed to be evacuated. With no thought for his own safety, Clarence jumped into his vehicle and rushed to help them. He drove through three feet of standing water and moved them to safety. Then Clarence mobilized five other vehicles and hurried to the coastline to rescue the injured. Sadly, few were injured; most were dead. On the first day alone, Clarence moved some seventy-five bodies. In the days that followed, he worked twenty-hour days burying the dead. He told me that what he witnessed that day will forever haunt him: the bodies of men, women, and children battered and twisted, strewn across the beach, trapped inside of homes, and draped in trees. Clarence is one of my heroes. This humble man of God was thrust by circumstance into something

After a tsunami struck Sri Lanka in late 2004, Clarence worked twenty-hour shifts and did whatever he could to help others.

horrible, and he responded by doing whatever he could to help his fellow man.

Hebrews 11 has been called the "Faith Hall of Fame" because it recounts the heroism of people throughout Scripture who paid a great price for their faith. Clarence is just such a hero of the faith—not only because he rose to the challenge on that day, but also because he laid down his life in the service of Christ years earlier. Clarence was there that day because he had long ago committed his life to serving God, whatever the cost. The writer of Hebrews said of these heroes that "the world was not worthy of them" (11:38).

Thankfully, many such heroes serve Christ today, and not just in faraway places like Sri Lanka, but in places right where God has placed you. Today's heroes of the faith can be found working with youth in the inner city, comforting the dying in hospice care, supporting a struggling single mother, spending their time with a disabled child, or visiting each day with an elderly shut-in. Each one of us can be a hero for Christ if we intentionally seek to imitate Christ's compassion and love for people. But we have to be willing to pay the price. You see, heroism always comes with a cost.

Boats were swept several miles inland in Banda Aceh, Indonesia, when the tsunami struck. More than 230,000 lives in fourteen countries were lost.

—RICH

STANDING ON
THE PROMISES

TAKE GOD AT HIS WORD AND ACT!

Command those who are rich in this present world not
to be arrogant nor to put their hope in wealth, which
is so uncertain, but to put their hope in God, who
richly provides us with everything for our enjoyment.
Command them to do good, to be rich in good deeds, and
to be generous and willing to share. In this way . . . they
may take hold of the life that is truly life.

I TIMOTHY 6:17–19

HAVE YOU EVER READ something in the newspaper and thought to
yourself, *Why in the world would anyone do that?* Maybe it was a story
about one of those competitive eaters, or the account of a man who hit a
golf ball across the entire width of Mongolia, or the woman who performed
thirty-five consecutive cartwheels on top of a kayak. Some things are just
too outrageous to comprehend.

Maybe that was how Abraham felt when God called him to sacrifice his
son Isaac. What a terrible idea! How many years had Abraham and Sarah

A family in rural Romania encounters a gaggle of geese.

waited for a child? How many times had God promised Abraham that he would be the father of many nations, that his offspring would be as numerous as the stars in the sky and the sand on the shore? Why, then, would God want Abraham to present his only son as a burnt offering? And yet, as inexplicable as God's command seemed, Abraham was willing to obey. So the very next morning, he got up, saddled his donkey, and took off for the place God had called him to go. He took the wood, he took the fire, and he took Isaac, the sacrifice. This was Abraham's opportunity to demonstrate his confidence in the promises of God. By giving up the thing he valued most in life, he was taking God at His word and acting on it.

It occurs to me that every time we reach out to those in need, every time we say a prayer or write a check or send a letter, we are demonstrating our faith in the promises of God. We are acting on our belief that God cares for the least of those in our world and that He will use our small offerings to make a difference.

New windows keep out the cold Romanian winter.

For several years, our family sponsored a family living in Romania, and every few months we received a letter from them. Mr. and Mrs. Rostas lived with their five children in a one-room house in a rural community outside of Cluj. One December we received a letter telling us that the family's Christmas celebration would be especially sweet that year because our sponsorship had enabled them to purchase a door and windows. The next Christmas they told us about the new floor they were able to install.

Encouraged, the following year, we sent an additional gift above and beyond our yearly sponsorship. Do you know how the Rostas family used that money? They gave at least some of it to the other children in their school whose families were also very poor. Every child received a gift because we did something the world might think of as foolish. We didn't invest that money in the stock market or in real estate, which at the time seemed prudent but in retrospect may have been a waste. Instead, we invested it in the lives of the Rostas family. We took God at His word: we believed His promises, and we acted.

—RENEÉ

A FATHER'S LOVE

WE ARE ALL CHILDREN OF GOD, DEEPLY LOVED BY HIM. AND HIS LOVE IS ENOUGH TO OVERCOME EVERYTHING.

See what great love the Father has lavished on us, that we should be called children of God! And that is what we are!

I JOHN 3:1

"TODAY MY FATHER ARRIVES. I don't know him. He says I am not his daughter." These were the words of nineteen-year-old Ruth on the day I met her in Tiraque, Bolivia. She hoped to meet her father for the first time later that day, the father who had abandoned her even before she was born. She was excited but also apprehensive.

In my work, I meet so many people who have been dealt a terrible hand in life, people who are sick, lame, abused, forgotten, and among the poorest of the poor—and I am always inspired by their determination to overcome. Ruth ranks high on my list of overcomers. She and her seven siblings were raised by her mother and stepfather in poverty, but Ruth did not let that keep her from setting goals for her life. Ruth had been part of our youth leadership program. She and the other teenagers had organized and successfully petitioned the government to open a legal clinic where abused women and children could receive help. That's when her dream was born: to someday be a lawyer and help women and children who are abused.

But when Ruth's parents told her she had to quit school and work in the city, her hopes were crushed. After months working as a maid, she returned home only to face another challenge: her family was moving to Argentina. Ruth could go with them, but she would again have to quit school and work. So, at just sixteen, she had decided to stay in Tiraque to finish school even though it meant she would be completely on her own.

As Ruth and I talked, I told her about my own nineteen-year-old daughter, Grace, and how, as a father, I loved her and helped her pursue her dreams. I told her that this is what fathers are supposed to do. That's when she broke my heart. "I have never known the love of a father," she said. Later that day, when Ruth went to meet her father, he never showed up.

Many of us have been let down by earthly fathers and mothers; all of us have suffered setbacks and trials. Have you been hurt, abused, mistreated,

Although she was abandoned as a child in Bolivia, Ruth draws strength from her heavenly Father.

A father near Cuddalore, India, holds his precious daughter.

or abandoned by someone you trusted? Perhaps, like Ruth, your dreams have been hobbled by a long series of disappointments.

Ruth never did experience the love of her earthly father, but she did know the love of her heavenly Father. He had kept her in His loving arms and kept her dream alive. "Somehow I'll make it," she told me. "I don't know how, but I know God is with me. God made me. He has a purpose in my trials."

Against all odds, Ruth finished high school and enrolled in the university to pursue law. You see, Ruth is a child of the King and deeply loved by Him. She has a Father who cherishes her. And so do you.

—RICH

I HOPE YOU DANCE

GOD CAN TURN ANY EXPERIENCE INTO AN OPPORTUNITY FOR REJOICING.

You turned my wailing into dancing;
you removed my sackcloth and clothed me with joy,
that my heart may sing to you and not be silent.
O LORD my God, I will give you thanks forever.

PSALM 30:11–12

DESPITE MANY YEARS of childhood ballet lessons, I am not, by anyone's definition, a dancer. But dancing is such an integral part of many cultures that, when we travel, I am often called upon to join in, which is fine, since it breaks the ice and gives those watching a reason to chuckle. In fact, if I listen quietly enough, I believe I can hear people in faraway places still laughing at that funny woman who couldn't seem to put one foot in front of the other.

Although they live in circumstances that would not make me feel like dancing, I encounter girls and boys, men and women everywhere rising up to dance at the slightest excuse for a celebration. This is particularly true in Malawi, known to visitors as "The Warm Heart of Africa." In the community of Chingale, a spontaneous conga line formed as women circled a shallow pond where tilapia was being farmed. So great was their joy at having food for their families and a product to sell in the market that they

Nigerien girls celebrate a new village well, which creates time for them to go to school and to play.

couldn't contain themselves. And they conscripted into their dance several of us whose only experience with tilapia was on a plate at Red Lobster.

Malawi was in the grip of a terrible food crisis due to drought, famine, and government efforts to reduce the country's dependence on agriculture. Children were suffering. But in this little community, a World Vision agricultural specialist had helped the people start a fish farm, and the dancing women were hardly able to contain their happiness.

Their celebration made me think of King David's reference to dancing in Psalm 30. It's believed to have been written in response to the incident recorded in 1 Chronicles 21:1–22:6. David had become overconfident in his ability to lead Israel and, in direct disobedience to God's command, ordered that his military leaders count his troops. Confronted by the prophet Gad, David acknowledged his sin and willingly submitted to God's discipline. Although the discipline was very painful, David later praised God, thanking Him for His mercy and restoration.

When life is hard, it's easy to get discouraged and overlook the ways God might be at work in our lives. A fishpond may not seem much to get excited about, but the people of Chingale didn't see it that way at all. Rather, they believed God had intervened in their lives in a way that filled them with so much joy they couldn't keep their feet from moving. David felt that way too. God turned the repentant king's mourning into dancing.

What is your response when you hit a bump in the road either of your own making or as the result of circumstances beyond your control? Do you despair, or do you dance? I'm reminded of the country song Lee Ann Womack sings: *Promise me that you'll give faith a fighting chance / And when you get the choice to sit it out or dance / I hope you dance.*

When was the last time you went dancing?

—RENEÉ

A SMILE
WITHOUT LIPS

THE POWER OF FORGIVENESS IS THE GREATEST SOURCE OF HEALING.

*"Whenever you stand praying, forgive, if you have
anything against anyone, so that your Father also who is
in heaven may forgive you your trespasses."*

JESUS IN MARK 11:25 ESV

DO YOU NEED TO FORGIVE SOMEONE?

Has someone done something hurtful to you? Jesus understood that one of man's most universal faults is that we keep a record of wrongs and we tend to hold grudges. That is why He so often told us to forgive and not to judge, lest we be judged by the same measure. It is unavoidable: in the course of our daily life, other people will say and do things that are hurtful. And so we keep our ledgers and remember each small sleight and every hurtful word sent our way. Over time, these accumulated grievances cripple our relationships—not just with friends, neighbors, and coworkers, but with our spouse, our children, and our family. Scar tissue builds up to the point of incapacitating these relationships. Like the ghost of Jacob Marley in *A Christmas Carol,* who

The people of Northern Uganda have prayed for years for peace and reconciliation. The ability to forgive such horrific wrongs can come only from the source of all forgiveness—Jesus.

shambled around dragging behind him the heavy chains and padlocks of his sins, we also drag our relational baggage behind us into our home, church, neighborhood, and workplace. That is why Jesus told us not to judge, but to forgive and to keep our slates clean. Forgiveness is a powerful medicine.

Margaret, a young wife and mother in Uganda, is a beautiful example of the power of forgiveness. In fact, I don't think I have ever seen forgiveness demonstrated more radically. When she was pregnant and working in the garden one day with her neighbors, the LRA attacked the women, murdering everyone but Margaret. It was bad luck to kill a pregnant woman, so they mutilated her instead: they cut off her ears, nose, and lips and left her to die. But she lived.

Horribly disfigured, Margaret lived and gave birth to her son, James, a few months after. Then, abandoned by her husband, she and her son went to live at World Vision's rehabilitation center in Gulu, also a place where the child soldiers who escaped the LRA went to be healed. Several months later a new batch of LRA soldiers arrived for rehabilitation. One of them was the young man who had given the order to mutilate Margaret.

When she saw him, Margaret became hysterical with fear, anger, and hatred. But after weeks of counseling and prayer, he was ready to ask forgiveness, and Margaret, tapping into the source of all forgiveness—Jesus—was finally ready to forgive. On that day, a photo was taken. It is a photo of Margaret and the man who maimed her. He is holding little James in his arms, and she is smiling. She is smiling without lips.

Forgiveness heals. Forgiveness removes scar tissue. Forgiveness transforms and empowers relationships. Has someone hurt you? Love them. Has someone insulted you? Compliment them. Has someone harmed you? Offer to help them. Has someone excluded you? Include them. Forgive them.

—Rich

WOMEN STAND
UP TOGETHER!

GOD CAN USE YOU TO BRING HIS HEALING INTO THE LIFE OF SOMEONE AROUND YOU.

When Jesus saw their faith, he said to the paralytic,
"Son, your sins are forgiven."

MARK 2:5

THE STATISTICS DON'T BEGIN to tell the real story of what is going on in the Democratic Republic of the Congo (DRC). Even when we hear that a thousand women are raped every day or that 1.7 million people have fled their homes to escape the fighting, the numbers fail to communicate the daily horrors experienced by ordinary Congolese women like Marie*.

Sixteen-year-old Marie sits in a wheelchair, paralyzed from the waist down. In an attack that killed both her parents, she was left for dead by a group of men who assaulted her with knives. Her sister struggled to get Marie to a village where there was a doctor, but they had no access to private cars or ambulances, and because of Marie's wounds, the bus drivers would not allow them on board. Finally, a passing truck let them ride in the back, but when the truck broke

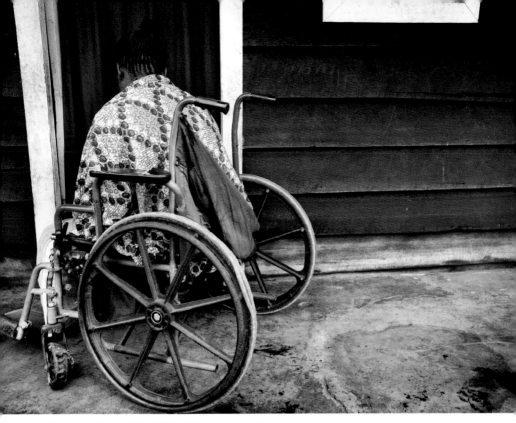

Living at a safe house in the DRC, Marie is strengthened by her sister's love.

down, the sisters were stranded on the side of the road. Time and again, efforts to get Marie to a doctor failed. When, after several days, Marie finally did see a doctor, the damage to her body was beyond repair. The two sisters now live together at the Wamama Simameni Safe House in Buhimba.

Mark 2 tells the story of another paralytic and his friends' valiant efforts to transport him to someone who could heal his broken body. Like Marie's sister, they too had trouble getting him to the One who could make him walk. The crowds were so large that the men couldn't bring their friend into the house where Jesus was preaching. But undeterred, they made an opening in the roof and lowered the paralytic down to the place where Jesus was standing. When Jesus saw not the paralytic's faith

A Congolese woman pours her heart out to God.

but the faith of his friends, He said to the young man lying on the mat, "Son, your sins are forgiven."

The Wamama Simameni Safe House is a bright light of hope and healing in an otherwise very dark place. The name means, "Women Stand Up Together," and that is exactly what is happening in this compound where victims of war have gathered to support and encourage one another. Marie's sister is one of the very few women who has not been physically assaulted, yet she refuses to leave. Her presence there is a powerful statement to Marie and the other victims that they will not be abandoned. Like the four men who refused to desert their paralyzed friend but with great effort took him to the true Source of healing, Marie's sister is willing to "stand up together" with the women of Wamama Simameni.

Who is God calling you to stand with today? Who can you, by your presence in that person's life, encourage and support? Remember how the influence of his friends changed the outcome of the paralytic's life. Who can you influence? Who can you take to the Healer?

—Reneé

SPIRITUAL DOMINOES

GOD USES THINGS WE OFTEN SEE AS UNIMPORTANT TO ACCOMPLISH VERY SIGNIFICANT THINGS.

"What do you think? If a man owns a hundred sheep, and one of them wanders away, will he not leave the ninety-nine on the hills and go to look for the one that wandered off? And if he finds it, truly I tell you, he is happier about that one sheep than about the ninety-nine that did not wander off. In the same way your Father in heaven is not willing that any of these little ones should perish."

JESUS IN MATTHEW 18:12–14

I DISCOVERED A DEEPLY profound insight in a very unlikely place last year. I was watching the kitschy *America's Got Talent* TV show when a character called the Kinetic King came on to perform. His shtick was arranging tens of thousands of sticks, cups, and dominoes to create spectacular chain reactions. And that's when it came to me: *A sweeping and profound series of events can begin with the falling of a single domino.* God—forgive me for the comparison—like the Kinetic King, works

Like this energetic schoolboy in Kenya, all children should have the chance to soar as high as they can.

through spiritual chain reactions in His church. He takes the seemingly insignificant acts and decisions of His followers and uses them to accomplish amazing things.

In 1979, then World Vision president Stan Mooneyham was passionate about helping the thousands of refugees—called the "boat people" at the time—who were fleeing Vietnam, Laos, and Cambodia. Though many people advised against it, Mooneyham decided to buy a boat, sail to the South China Sea, and rescue some of the thousands who were perishing there while the rest of the world just watched. By most standards the mission was a failure. He was only really able to rescue just one boatload of a few hundred souls fleeing Vietnam. In violation of international law, the boat picked them up and took them to safety at a refugee camp for processing.

Vinh Chung was a four-year-old boy on that boat. He was rescued along with his parents and seven siblings. The first domino fell. The Chung family was processed and ultimately given asylum in the United

States and resettled in Arkansas. Another domino fell. Then a local Baptist church adopted the Chungs and helped them acclimate, provided for some of their needs, and worked with them to learn English. Mr. Chung found work in a factory and earned enough to move his family of thirteen into a three-bedroom house. Every member of the family became a Christian and began attending the church. More dominoes fell. Little Vinh, now with ten brothers and sisters, began to flourish and did very well in school.

Fast forward a few decades. Vinh was accepted at Harvard. Then he attended Harvard Medical School. He married Liesel, another Asian immigrant he had met in high school, who got her MBA from Harvard Business School. Today Vinh and Liesel have three children, and they both work in Vinh's medical practice in Colorado. Every one of Vinh's siblings went to college, and most have advanced graduate degrees from the best universities. Vinh now serves on the World Vision US board of directors. Vinh and Liesel are also now generous donors to

Every child is made in the image of God and brimming with possibilities.

World Vision's ministry, because they understand the power of a simple act of kindness. They understand the power of falling dominoes.

Jesus once said, "If anyone gives even a cup of cold water to one of these little ones who is my disciple, truly I tell you, that person will certainly not lose their reward." What will you do with your domino?

—RICH

CONSTRUCTION PROJECT

BUILD YOUR LIFE ON JESUS CHRIST SO THAT WHEN TRIALS COME, YOU WILL BE ABLE TO STAND FIRM.

"I will show you what he is like who comes to me and hears my words and puts them into practice. He is like a man building a house, who dug down deep and laid the foundation on rock. When a flood came, the torrent struck the house but could not shake it, because it was well built."

JESUS IN LUKE 6:47–48

RECENTLY, MY SON ANDREW AND HIS WIFE purchased a house. While it had "good bones" and was located in a lovely neighborhood, it needed some work—a coat of paint, fixtures in the bathroom, and new floors to replace the dark green shag carpet. But they were willing to overlook these cosmetic flaws because the home inspection came back clean: the foundation was solid and the house was otherwise in good shape.

The little house George built for his brother and sister in the village of Senzani, Malawi was not. When George was twelve, his parents died of AIDS, and he became the sole caregiver for two younger siblings. When the family hut fell down because of a termite infestation, this young man—hardly more than a boy himself—rebuilt it on his own. "When I built this house," he told me, "I thought, *This is what my dad would have done.*" But it was obvious that termites were at it again. George once more faced the daunting task of rebuilding. Yet this time it would be easier. George and his siblings would have help. George's sister, Liveness, was a sponsored child, and they would have the support of others who would help them build on a stronger foundation.

Jesus told a parable about two men who set out to build houses. The wise builder chose solid rock as his foundation. When flood-

Left without parents, George built a life and a house for his brother and sister in Malawi.

waters came, his house stood firm. So it is, Jesus said, with the person who hears God's Word and puts it into practice. Whatever storms life brings, that person remains secure.

The foolish man, however, built his house on a foundation of sand. It was no match for stormy weather and the house quickly collapsed. He hadn't taken the time to dig deep beneath the surface. He opted for a quick and easy approach, and the resulting house lacked the strength to stand against the storm. Likewise, the person who hears God's Word and does not put it into practice builds his life on a shallow and temporary foundation. He builds on what ultimately will not stand against all that life throws his way.

Just before Jesus told the crowd this parable, He asked them, "Why do you call me 'Lord, Lord,' and do not do what I say?" (Luke 6:46). In

Homes in rural Malawi, built with mud and thatch, need a solid foundation.

other words, why do you hear My teachings but not put them into practice? Why do you claim to follow Me when your life makes it obvious that you've chosen something other than Me as your foundation?

The evidence is in the home inspection. Does your house look good on the surface, but further examination reveals the equivalent of termites or a cracked and crumbling foundation? Did you choose a quick and easy approach to building, not giving much attention to the surface upon which you've built? Have you constructed your life around your career, your family, your possessions, your church attendance? Or have you made Jesus and His Word your bedrock, so that whatever the weather, you can stand firm?

—Reneé

ARE YOU COMFORTABLE?

God calls us to step out of our comfort zone and get engaged.

Peter spoke up, "We have left everything to follow
you!" "Truly I tell you," Jesus replied, "no one who has
left home or brothers or sisters or mother or father or
children or fields for me and the gospel will fail to receive
a hundred times as much in this present age."

MARK 10:28–30

I ACTUALLY GOT up the courage last week to get into the swimming pool with my one-year-old grandson. Now, I hate getting into swimming pools because of that initial shock of cold water. But this swimming pool felt like bathwater. Not only was it easy to get in, it was so comfortable that it was hard to get out!

Sadly, our Christian faith can be just like that pool water—oh, so comfortable. Reading Scripture and praying during our quiet times can draw us closer to God, ease our fears, and calm our spirit. Our churches offer inspiring worship, nurturing community, and often a full selection of social activities ranging from spiritual retreats to moms' aerobic classes

After a flash flood in the Dominican Republic, a teen risks his life to save a child.

to organized mountain hikes. The water is just so warm and comfortable. Yet Jesus said, "Whoever wants to be my disciple must deny themselves and take up their cross and follow me . . . What good will it be for someone to gain the whole world, yet forfeit their soul?" (Matthew 16:24, 26).

With its incredibly beautiful and upscale neighborhoods, Falls Church, Virginia, can be a comfortable place too. But just a mile or so away, on the other side of town, is a world of youth gangs and violence, with lost kids desperately needing to be rescued from that road to destruction. Juan was one of those kids. After coming from El Salvador as a child, he drifted into a gang that offered him all the things your church offers you—minus God: family, friends, acceptance, love, and a sense of belonging. But Juan had traded his soul for all that. He got involved with crime and violence, saw his friend shot, and ended up in jail. But when he was released, he found help in an unlikely place. He got a job at a restaurant, and the manager treated Juan with respect, trusted him, and gave him a chance. In Juan's words, "She knew how to forgive and forget. She looked at me as a human being."

And that was what Juan needed to get his life back on track. He got back into school, earned his degree, and was then offered a position with a nonprofit. The job? Going back into the gang neighborhood as a counselor to help rescue lost kids from that lifestyle—and Juan was terrified. These were the same gangs that had shot at him just a few years earlier. "Fear sometimes stops good people from doing the right thing," Juan said. But Juan did the right thing and spent the next few years counseling kids and speaking in high schools.

I can guarantee that lost kids and desperate people live within a couple of miles of your church and your home. And just as Jesus came to rescue you and me, they need someone to rescue them. That's one reason why, when we follow Jesus, He calls us to take up our cross and follow Him into the broken and ragged places in our world. He asks us to join the rescue mission. "Sometimes," Juan said, "it takes being uncomfortable." Are you too comfortable?

—RICH

WALK A MILE IN
MY SHOES!

**JUST AS JESUS STEPPED INTO OUR LIVES, WE NEED TO STEP
INTO THE LIVES OF THOSE AROUND US.**

*Christ Jesus, who, being in very nature God, did not
consider equality with God something to be grasped,
but made himself nothing, taking the very nature of a
servant, being made in human likeness.*

PHILIPPIANS 2:5–7

WHEN I WAS ASKED TO GIVE A SPEECH about the importance of
clean water, I was nervous. What did I know about what life is like for the
more than 783 million people around the world who have no access to safe
water? To prepare, I decided to conduct an experiment: for twenty-four
hours, I turned off the tap.

I know the experiment was limited. For me, no running water only
meant a bad hair day, a long walk to the beach carrying a turquoise blue
Rubbermaid bucket, and the struggle to return home without spilling all
the water out of my bucket and onto my sneakers. But that day gave me a
new appreciation for those for whom the struggle to find water isn't just an
experiment but is a matter of life or death.

After all, most childhood diseases are related to water, hygiene, and sanitation. In fact, worldwide, one child dies every minute as a result of illnesses associated with drinking dirty water, most of them before their fifth birthday. Little Faouzia is at risk of becoming one of these statistics. She lives with her family in Niger, a landlocked country on the edge of the Sahara Desert, where—according to UNICEF—41 percent of the population lacks access to clean water. Two-year-old Faouzia weighs scarcely fifteen pounds, and the sores in her mouth make it hard for her to swallow the little bit of food her mother, Zeinabou, has to give her. Zeinabou told me Faouzia has been sick since birth, but making matters worse is the fact that the water her big sister, Rakia, brings home for the family comes from a fetid pond outside the village. Every morning, as she draws water, Rakia stands in waste-contaminated water beside animals brought to drink, bathe, and cool themselves at the tainted watering hole.

Street children in Goma, DRC, wait to receive new shoes and clothing.

Women walk for miles after drawing water from a filthy pond in Ghana.

Clearly, my little experiment didn't get me anywhere close to experiencing what Zeinabou and her family go through every day. But I do think I had the right idea. In my small, limited way, I at least tried to put myself in their shoes.

When you think about it, isn't that what Jesus did for us? "The Word became flesh and made his dwelling among us" (John 1:14). God stepped into our shoes. Shouldn't we be willing to do the same for our brothers and sisters around the world? At the very least, when we take a shower, we should stop and pray for those who will never bathe in anything but a muddy pond. When we give our children a glass of water, we should pray with them for children who ingest life-threatening parasites whenever they take a drink. When we brush our teeth, do the laundry, or wash the dishes, we should pray, knowing that many people can't do what we take for granted. Christ identified with humanity—to the point that it cost Him His life. Lord, *give me strength to follow Your example.*

—RENEÉ

LEARNING FROM SCROOGE

OUR LIVES CAN BE TRANSFORMED WHEN WE INVEST IN THE LIVES OF OTHERS.

"See that you do not look down on one of these little ones. For I tell you that their angels in heaven always see the face of my Father in heaven."

JESUS IN MATTHEW 18:10

"Spirit," said Scrooge, with an interest he had never felt before, "tell me if Tiny Tim will live." "I see a vacant seat," replied the Ghost, "in the poor chimney-corner, and a crutch without an owner, care-fully preserved. If these shadows remain unaltered by the Future, the child will die." "No, no," said Scrooge. "Oh, no, kind Spirit. Say he will be spared."

—CHARLES DICKENS, *A CHRISTMAS CAROL*

ONE OF MY FAVORITE HOLIDAY STORIES is Charles Dickens's *A Christmas Carol*. It endures as a timeless story of hope—the hope embodied in the spirit of Tiny Tim and the hope newly kindled in the hardened heart of Ebenezer Scrooge. Tiny Tim, like so many of the

Like Charles Dickens's Tiny Tim, impoverished children such as these two in Zambia are often playful and hopeful despite the poverty that surrounds them.

children I meet around the world, had a sunny disposition and was rich in hopes and dreams despite his crippling handicap and dreary circumstances. I have met many such children who, like Tiny Tim, often seem unaware of their own poverty and are grateful for the little they have.

In Uganda, I met three brothers orphaned by AIDS who dreamed of becoming a doctor, a teacher, and a pilot. I still can see the bright smile of eleven-year-old Sunshine, thrilled beyond description about moving into the new cinder block house built for her family in the Philippines. I will never forget my visit to a dump outside Manila and the sight of two little girls standing alone in fifty acres of garbage, giggling as they played house with a broken doll and empty pots and pans. And then there was the boy in Kenya who proudly showed me a treasured truck he had made from empty cans and chicken wire, perhaps the only toy he would ever know.

We can learn much from the innocent hopes of the Tiny Tims in our world, but what of old Scrooge? He was successful, wealthy, powerful, hard-working, and driven. He embodied the very characteristics we celebrate in our pursuit of the American dream. It isn't too much of a stretch to see glimpses of Scrooge in people we know well—and perhaps even in our-selves. In his quest for success, Scrooge was self-absorbed and oblivious to the real needs of the people around him—until he had that life-changing encounter with Jacob Marley's ghost. Scrooge saw in that dream not only what he could do to help others, but also how much joy was missing from his own life.

The magic of this story is that Scrooge and Tiny Tim ultimately found the fulfillment of their hopes in each other. Scrooge's life was transformed by the love of a child, and Tiny Tim's future was changed by Scrooge's generosity. *Scrooge was better than his word. He did it all, and infinitely more; and to Tiny Tim, who did not die, he was a second father.*

If the ghost of Jacob Marley could jolt Scrooge into changing his life, shouldn't our encounter with Jesus have an even greater impact on us? The One who bade His disciples to "welcome these little children" in His name also bids us to welcome the Tiny Tims of the world into our hearts.

—RICH

A boy in Burundi decorated his handmade toy truck with World Vision logos.

THE HANDS AND FEET OF CHRIST

YOU MAY BE THE ONLY JESUS SOME PEOPLE WILL EVER MEET.

"As you sent me into the world, I have
sent them into the world."

JESUS IN JOHN 17:18

YOU MAY HAVE HEARD THE STATEMENT, "You may be the only Jesus some people ever see." It makes the point that as followers of Christ, we bear the responsibility of demonstrating to the world what Jesus might look like were He to walk the earth today. Those who will never enter the door of a church or read a Bible or hear a sermon can still know Jesus by watching us! I'm not sure I always give others the right impression, but I met someone who does.

Tseghe, a fourteen-year-old Ethiopian girl, was abducted by a stranger as she walked to school. Because the man lacked money to pay the bride price, he simply stole Tseghe from the side of the road, intending to make her his wife. He took her shoes so she couldn't run and marched her miles from her home to a shack where he bound and assaulted her.

Although everyone in the village heard what had happened, no one came to her aid. "She's damaged goods," they said. "Leave well enough

A rescued Tseghe at home with her grandmother in Ethiopia.

alone. That's just the way things are. If you can't afford a bride, you just take one."

But Tseghe's grandmother was determined to find her, and she recruited Esatu, a World Vision staff member, to help. When Esatu first went to the police, they refused to act. But he persisted, and over the course of the next several days, Tseghe was found and returned home.

I asked the older woman what Esatu's efforts had meant to her. "It would have been enough," she said, "if he had just come alongside me and been my friend, but he did so much more."

In that instant, my mind flashed to another desert in another country and a stable in a town called Bethlehem. Looking at the Creator of the universe lying helpless in a manger, some might say it would have been enough had Jesus simply come alongside us to be our Friend. But of course, that wasn't enough at all, because more than a friend to walk

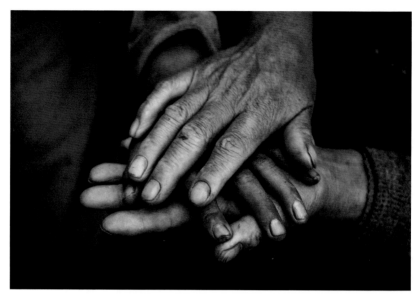
Christians are called to be the hands of Christ.

beside us, more than an example to follow, what we really needed was a Savior.

Esatu had already done plenty. He'd worked hard to provide for the needs of the community, and rescuing Tseghe wasn't his responsibility. But that thought never crossed his mind. When Esatu came to the aid of a young girl and her desperate grandmother, he was just doing what Jesus would have done if He had been there on that terrible day.

And in a way, Jesus was. Esatu's hands were Jesus' hands; Esatu's heart was Jesus' heart. When wicked men sought to steal away a young girl's dignity and hope for the future, Jesus came to Tseghe's rescue in the person of a man named Esatu.

Is there someone you know who needs Jesus, someone to whom you can demonstrate through your friendship, your encouragement, your wise counsel, the love of the Savior? Look at the people around you. You just might be the only Jesus they will ever see.

—RENEÉ

INDOOR PLUMBING

JESUS WANTS US TO THIRST FOR GOD JUST AS WE THIRST FOR WATER, AND HE OFFERS US "LIVING WATER": HIS SPIRIT WHO WILL SATISFY OUR DEEPEST THIRST.

On the last and greatest day of the Feast, Jesus stood and said in a loud voice, "If anyone is thirsty, let him come to me and drink. Whoever believes in me, as the Scripture has said, streams of living water will flow from within him." By this he meant the Spirit, whom those who believed in him were later to receive. Up to that time the Spirit had not been given, since Jesus had not yet been glorified.

JOHN 7:37–39

HOW WOULD YOUR LIFE CHANGE IF, tomorrow morning, your community no longer had water? After your panic subsided, the urgent search for water would immediately become your number-one priority, pushing aside everything else—work, school, family, relationships, recreation, even your need for food.

In Bible times, centuries before the advent of indoor plumbing, every family's top priority was to seek out and secure their water. This task required hours of work and backbreaking labor, but without water a family and their animals would perish. So when Jesus invited people

A schoolgirl in Ghana enjoys clean water from a borehole in her village.

to come and drink from "streams of living water," every one of His first-century listeners understood the incredible offer He was making. After all, they understood thirst at a visceral, life-or-death level.

In Africa there is a saying: "Water is life." Water is not important for life; it literally *is* life. Whenever a new well is drilled, hundreds of people turn out to see the rig strike water. When that first gusher comes out of the ground, there is great rejoicing: people dance, sing, and offer prayers of thanksgiving. When I visited a village in Ghana a few years back, the people regaled me with stories of how a new well of living water in their village had changed their lives. Child mortality had plummeted, school attendance had increased tenfold, women now had time for more productive work, sickness had declined, and productivity had risen. I spoke to one woman who said through her tears that now, for the first time in her thirty-five years of life, she and her children did not have to make the seven-mile round trip twice each day to fetch water. Her all-consuming quest for water was now over.

Jesus' offer of living water means that our quest can be over too. He wants us to thirst for God in that same life-and-death way we thirst for water, yet He promised that when we put our faith in Him, we will never thirst again. Never again will we have to wander in a spiritual desert searching for that which can sustain our human souls. Jesus quenches our spiritual thirst by filling us with His Holy Spirit, who is like a stream of living water flowing within us. Jesus was offering indoor plumbing to those who had never had it: "Everyone who drinks this water will be thirsty again, but whoever drinks the water I give them will never thirst" (John 4:13–14).

This is a remarkable gift. As Christians, baptized in the Holy Spirit, we now have God literally dwelling within us. This "spring of living water" (Jeremiah 17:13) perpetually satisfies us as we take our hurts and our needs, our hopes and our dreams, and our spiritual hunger and thirst directly to God. We have new and complete access to God's truth, to His comfort, and to His power. Our quest is over.

—RICH

IT'S A BIG WORLD
OUT THERE

To stay connected to what God is doing in the world, we need to stay connected to Him.

As for me, it is good to be near God.

PSALM 73:28

UNTIL RICH AND I BECAME INVOLVED in the work of World Vision, I had a pretty limited perspective on the world around me, and if we're being honest, I think that's true of most Americans. We live in a world only as large as our own personal experiences. And if the way I spend my time is any indication, I often act as if my world were only the size of the space between my house, the grocery store, the mall, and my church!

But the truth is, it's a big world out there, and it can often feel like we're a long way from what's happening on the other side. We find it hard to imagine what it's like for people living without clean water, accessible medical care, or a roof over their heads. And it can be a greater challenge to believe we have any role to play in making life better for those living on the edge. Our perspective is limited. We lack the big picture.

A similar situation faced the people Nehemiah recruited to restore the wall around Jerusalem (Nehemiah 2:17–18). Finding the wall in ruins, he

People arrive at dawn to pray for hours before a church service in Ethiopia.

assigned families to rebuild only that section of the wall right in front of their own house. They couldn't see what was going on around the curve, on the other side of the city, or even a hundred yards away.

However, they all knew there was one person who could see the big picture, one person who knew firsthand the progress that was being made. Every day Nehemiah traveled around the whole city to survey the work. If someone wasn't working fast enough, or didn't build straight enough, or had decided to change the style of the wall, Nehemiah took care of it. When men opposed the rebuilding of the wall, Nehemiah had a plan. When they stirred up trouble, he had a solution. Because the people trusted Nehemiah, they didn't worry but instead continued to do the work he had assigned to them.

In the same way that the people of Jerusalem stayed connected to the rebuilding project by staying connected to Nehemiah, we can stay connected to God's work in the world by staying connected to Him, by spending time in worship, in fellowship, in God's Word, and in prayer. E. M. Bounds, a nineteenth-century Methodist minister, wrote this: "The men who have most fully illustrated Christ in their character and have most powerfully affected the world for Him, have been men who spend so much time with God as to make it a notable feature in their lives."

If you're uncertain about your place in the work God is doing in the world, make sure you're staying connected to Him. Are you willing to do what God puts right in front of you? Are worship and prayer and the reading of God's Word notable features in your life? If so, then you can trust God for the big picture, knowing that He has a place for you to serve!

—RENEÉ

Sunday morning mass is held in an impoverished community in Turkana, Kenya.

THE WORLD'S SHORTEST SERMON

GOD CALLS US TO CHANGE OUR LIVES.

After John was arrested, Jesus went to Galilee preaching
the Message of God: "Time's up! God's kingdom is here.
Change your life and believe the Message."

MARK 1:14–15 MSG

WITH ITS SIXTY-SIX BOOKS, almost two thousand pages, and a zillion impossible-to-pronounce names, the Bible can seem complex and confusing. Yet Jesus' first recorded words in the gospel of Mark were a sermon of less than fifteen words—and they summarized Jesus' entire message.

First, Jesus announced the incredibly good news that, through Him, the doors of God's kingdom had been flung open, and everyone could now enter into a different way of living in relationship to God. Then Jesus told us how to make that happen: by first believing His message and then by changing our life. Most translations use the word *repent* in this verse, but that doesn't really capture the original notion from the Greek. A more literal translation would be to change one's mind, to make a 180-degree turn, to base one's whole life on this new reality. It is essentially a call to

After years of living on the street, the gospel message transformed the life of Johnny and his family in Bolivia.

first believe the good news and to then spend the rest of our life becoming more like Jesus.

The great pastor and theologian John Stott wrote these words near the end of his life: "God wants his people to become like Christ, for Christlikeness is the will of God for the people of God." The beauty of Jesus' message is that it is deep enough for the most brilliant theologian, but also simple enough for a five-year-old child. And this message has the power to transform anyone's life.

I could offer countless examples of this life-changing power, but let me share just one. I met a man named Johnny in Bolivia, and if anyone needed hope and change, it was Johnny. His mother died when he was seven, shortly after that his father abandoned him, and Johnny was forced to live on the streets. The result was predictable: drugs, alcoholism, gangs, and crime. Johnny married a teenage girl and had three children, but his alcoholism, frequent outbursts of anger, and violence hung over his family like a dark cloud—until this message of Jesus grabbed hold of his life: "Time's up, Johnny! Change your life and believe the Message." The gospel came to Johnny through a pastor named Gerson who ran a counseling program for couples in trouble.

The gospel message changed Johnny. When I spoke with this new Johnny, I asked him to describe how he had changed. "I told the pastor what I was like, and he told me to put God first overall. He said, 'You have to be different. You have to change.' And so I took his advice for serious, and since then I am no longer like I used to be."

This is the message of Jesus for us as well. We need to believe the good news, "take his advice for serious," and "no longer be like we used to be."

—RICH

Children race through fields of flowers in Mexico.

MORE BLESSINGS

HOW WE RESPOND TO THE HARDSHIPS THAT COME INTO OUR LIVES IS REALLY UP TO US.

"This day I call heaven and earth as witnesses against you that I have set before you life and death, blessings and curses. Now choose life, so that you and your children may live."

DEUTERONOMY 30:19

"DON'T SAY I NEVER TAKE YOU ANYWHERE," Rich jokes when we travel to some of the more unusual places World Vision works. One that stands out in my mind is a brothel in Livingston, Zambia. We sat outside on hard wooden benches under a glaring spotlight, waiting with a young girl for her first client of the evening. She was fifteen, forced into prostitution in order to provide for her aging grandmother and disabled uncle. Hardly more than a child herself, she cradled in her arms her newborn daughter, ironically named More Blessings.

World Vision's offer to teach her a trade had not been enough to persuade her to quit. Not even the promise of a new sewing machine when she graduated from an alternative skills class had been adequate to convince her to abandon this lucrative trade. Rich and I were also unable to get her to change her mind, so at the end of the evening, we reluctantly left her and her

A baby in Niger swings in a cradle.

Former sex workers embrace a new life in the DRC.

baby behind at the brothel. But I couldn't get the child's name—More Blessings—out of my mind. *Why did she call this child, the product of some nameless liaison, More Blessings?* It implied that she had already been blessed, but looking at her present situation, I found it hard to see how that could possibly be true.

Somehow, this young woman seemed to know what so many of us struggle to comprehend: what may at first seem a bitter trial may actually be used by God to bring blessings into our lives. Early in our marriage, my husband lost his job—twice. A challenge for the father of five little kids? You bet. But it drove Rich to the cross in a way nothing else ever would. And when I was diagnosed with a serious illness, I experienced the steadfast love of the Lord in a manner that I might otherwise have missed. I don't pretend to know the burdens others bear, but I do know that it has been during some of my darkest times that I have been most keenly aware of God's presence in my life.

At the end of Moses' life, he stood before the people of Israel and reminded them that they had a choice to make: They could decide to follow God or they could reject Him. They could obey Him or turn away. They could choose life, or they could choose death. The choice was theirs.

More Blessing's mom also had a choice to make. In a life full of hardship, she chose to see this child as evidence of God's willingness to break into her pain and suffering and to bless her. How do you respond when hardships come your way? What choices do you make? Do you shake your fist at God and give in to anger and despair? Or do you see hardships as opportunities to draw closer to Him and allow Him to begin a new work in your life?

—Reneé

HAVE YOU ENLISTED?

GOD CALLS US TO LAY DOWN OUR LIVES BY ENLISTING IN HIS SERVICE AND LIVING FOR HIM.

For I am already being poured out like a drink offering, and the time for my departure is near. I have fought the good fight, I have finished the race, I have kept the faith.

2 TIMOTHY 4:6–7

ENLISTING IN THE MILITARY is a pretty radical form of commitment to serve one's country. It requires more than almost any other vocation. Think about it. When you enlist, you relinquish control over just about every dimension of your life: where you live, what you do, when you do it, even the clothes you wear. You fully embrace the mission of the country you serve, agreeing even to lay down your life if required.

More than most people I have ever known, Virginia enlisted, not in the military, but in her service to Christ. Virginia grew up in poverty in rural Peru. But after some help from our organization, she overcame her difficult background, studied to become a nurse, and began serving about fifteen hundred sponsored children in the mountain villages near Calqui Central, two and a half miles above sea level. When Reneé and I met her, she was

Dr. Maria Lorena Orellana returned to her rural community in Bolivia to serve the poor.

single, living a Spartan existence, and deliberately forgoing the comfort of the city and the opportunities her nursing skills would offer her there. Filling her backpack with medical supplies, she'd head into the mountains for up to ten days at a time, hiking from village to village to help the women and children. Virginia carried no sleeping bag or tent; she simply slept wherever she could—on a floor, under a tree, even out in the open. It was a hard life, especially for a young woman.

Virginia led Reneé and me high into the mountains to meet the women and children she calls her friends. She loves them and knows them all by name. We saw her weep as she hugged and consoled a recently widowed mother of three. Virginia has sacrificed everything in her life to help the poor in her country. She told us that she never felt real love until she committed her life to Christ. Now she wants others to feel His love: "This is my service," she told us. "This is not a job. It is my sacrifice, my life that I give to Christ."

Jesus said, "Whoever does not take up their cross and follow me is not worthy of me. Whoever finds their life will lose it, and whoever loses their life for my sake will find it" (Matthew 10:38–39)—and this is a hard teaching. Jesus spoke not about literally losing our lives, but rather about giving our lives *to* Him and living our lives *for* Him. How do you see your life as a follower of Christ? Perspective is everything. Is it yours to do with as you please, or is it God's to do with as He pleases? Shouldn't the call to follow Christ be even more radical than enlisting in the military? Have you lost your life for His sake, as Virginia did—that you might now truly find it?

> *Take my life, and let it be*
> *Consecrated, Lord, to Thee;*
> *Take my moments and my days,*
> *Let them flow in ceaseless praise;*
> *Let them flow in ceaseless praise.*

—FRANCES R. HAVERGAL, *TAKE MY LIFE AND LET IT BE*

—RICH

UGANDA

FOLLOWING THE
SHEPHERD

GOD GIVES US COURAGE TO SERVE OTHERS WHEN WE ALLOW
THEIR NEEDS TO LAY CLAIM TO OUR LIVES.

*"The man who loves his life will lose it, while the man
who hates his life in this world will keep it for eternal
life. Whoever serves me must follow me; and where I
am, my servant also will be."*

JESUS IN JOHN 12:25–26

ON A TABLE IN THE ENTRYWAY of our house sits a small wooden carving of a Ugandan fishing boat, a gift from a young woman named Margaret. Each day when I leave the house, it reminds me not only of my visit to Northern Uganda in 2006, but also of her extraordinary courage.

Margaret grew up in Northern Uganda, a place where for well over twenty-five years a brutal band of rebels from the LRA terrorized, tortured, and killed the peaceful Acholi people. It is a place where girls were abducted to be used as sex slaves, and boys were snatched away from their homes and forced to murder their friends and family. Too ashamed and afraid to return to their villages, they became part of Kony's little-boy army, used to perpetuate his reign of terror.

It was here that I met Margaret, a young woman who had taken it upon herself to lead a movement of reconciliation between her people and the rebel leader. Unlike many other young Ugandans, Margaret had managed to escape the worst horrors of the war. She was able to complete her education and get a job. Yet, despite the relative comfort in which she lived, she felt compelled to get involved. She arranged meetings with Kony's lieutenants. She testified before the United Nations. On her last visit to the States, I found her full of hope and excitement at

Demonstrators in Uganda call for peace and reconciliation in the home village of rebel leader Joseph Kony.

Margaret (left) gave her life to work for peace in Uganda.

the prospect of peace in her land. But less than a month after I saw her, Margaret was dead, poisoned as she ate lunch in a little cafe in Gulu. No one ever found out who was responsible.

Each time I met with Margaret, I marveled at her lack of animosity toward Joseph Kony and his rebels, and I was amazed at both her courage and her commitment to seek peace. Margaret was a twenty-six-year-old Acholi woman who, because of her education and hard work, had seemingly unlimited prospects for the future. She could have walked away from the horrors unfolding in Northern Uganda. She could have made a life for herself almost anywhere else in the world. And yet, as my pastor once said, she let the needs of her people lay claim to her life.

Each time I walk out the door, the little boat she gave me reminds me that I, too, must let the needs of others lay claim to my life. In all likelihood, I will never be called upon to make the ultimate sacrifice for another person, but I do need to hold loosely my time, my possessions, my relationships. Whatever it is that I value most, I need to be ready to relinquish it, to lay it down, to follow the example of Margaret—and of Jesus, who said, "I am the good shepherd. The good shepherd lays down his life for the sheep" (John 10:11).

—RENEÉ

WHO IS THIS JESUS?

In the beginning was the Word, and the Word was with God, and the Word was God. He was with God in the beginning. Through him all things were made; without him nothing was made that has been made. In him was life, and that life was the light of all mankind. The light shines in the darkness, and the darkness has not overcome it.

JOHN 1:1–5

ROTH WAS SUSPICIOUS. You would have been suspicious, too, if you had lived through the Khmer Rouge genocide in Cambodia in the 1970s. Pol Pot's ruthless forces had pillaged the countryside and killed one out of every five Cambodians—almost two million people! So when strangers from World Vision entered his community in the 1990s, Roth Ourng was suspicious and wary. The strangers set up a tuberculosis clinic, worked with the children in school, and taught farmers new agricultural techniques. But Roth did not trust them; he was convinced they had ulterior motives.

One day he decided to act on his suspicions. He confronted the program leader and demanded to know why he was there. The answer—"We

THIS PAGE AND FACING PAGE: After asking "Who is this Jesus?" Roth Ourng became a believer and went on to pastor a small church in Cambodia.

are followers of Jesus Christ, and we are commanded to love our neighbors"—was not what Roth expected to hear. "Who is this Jesus Christ?" Roth demanded. The leader gave Roth a Bible in the Khmer language and told him that he would find Jesus there. So Roth went home and began reading. "In the book of Genesis," he told me, "I found the God I had always wondered about, the God who created the world. But I still did not know who Jesus was, so I went back the next day to ask again."

"Who is this Jesus?" Roth was not the first to ask that question. Pilate also asked Jesus whether He was the king of the Jews (Matthew 27:11).

Thirty years earlier the wise men sought Him at His birth, and Herod the Great tried to kill Him (Matthew 2:1–13). The centurion who witnessed His crucifixion exclaimed, "Surely this man was the Son of God!" (Mark 15:39). Doubting Thomas fell at Jesus' feet saying, "My Lord and my God!" (John 20:26–28). Saul persecuted Jesus' followers until he met Him in a blinding light on the road to Damascus (Acts 9:1–5). John called Jesus the "light of all mankind" (John 1:4). Abraham Lincoln, Martin Luther King Jr., and Mother Teresa all followed Him. This Jesus demands a response.

God led Roth and a friend to a Cambodian pastor who explained that God had sent Jesus, His only begotten Son, to die so that they might live. Now Roth knew he, too, would have to decide about Jesus. The Son of God cannot be ignored. Either He becomes Lord of our life, or we remain Lord of our life. There is no other option.

When I met Roth, he was the pastor of a little house church with eighty-three members. When I asked where he had found so many members, he answered, "After I discovered Jesus, I had to tell everyone I knew. These are my sheep; this is my flock."

So who is this Jesus to you? There is no middle ground. When the fishermen, Peter and Andrew, met Jesus, "at once they left their nets and followed him" (Matthew 4:20). Jesus demands to be everything to us—or nothing. Which is He for you?

—Rich

PUSHING THE ELEPHANT

OUR FAITH DOES NOT MAKE US IMMUNE TO THE TROUBLES OTHERS SUFFER.

Do not think that because you are in the king's house you alone of all the Jews will escape. For if you remain silent at this time, relief and deliverance for the Jews will arise from another place, but you and your father's family will perish.

ESTHER 4:13–14

WE'D SPENT AN ENTIRE WEEK talking with women who'd been the victims of violence at the hands of warring militias. I was ready for a break, eager to meet with the Congolese women who worked for World Vision. We planned to watch the film *Pushing the Elephant,* the story of a mother who had managed to escape the DRC and her efforts to be reunited with the young daughter she had left behind. I was skeptical that it would resonate with the staff. But when, a few minutes into the movie the women dissolved into tears, it became clear that the story on the screen was, in some way, the story of the women in this room. Each one of these educated, professional, faith-filled women had been a victim in one way or another of the violence they saw portrayed.

Women in the DRC find strength in each other.

What was truly amazing to me was that none of these women had ever talked about their experiences with one another. Each morning they arrived at the office in makeup, high heels, and beautiful Congolese dress, never letting on about the troubles they had lived through. Maybe each of them assumed that the others in the office had been immune to the horrors she had suffered; that by virtue of education, privilege, or accomplishment, the other women had avoided the struggles she had faced.

Perhaps Esther, wife of Xerxes, ruler of the Persian Empire, thought at first that she was immune to the troubles her people faced. After all, she was queen, chosen for her beauty and favored among all the king's wives. But when Haman convinced Xerxes to issue a decree to destroy the Jews, Mordecai warned her cousin Esther that her position as queen would not protect her from the edict. Along with all the other Jews, she too would be killed by her husband's army. Esther alone, however, had a unique opportunity to speak to the king on behalf of her people.

When we read the story of Esther, we're reminded that, just as He strategically positioned Esther, God may have placed us where we are right now for a purpose, to accomplish something of His work in the world. That is an important reminder. But equally important is the idea that, as Mordecai told the queen, we are not immune to the pain and loss that others suffer. We may think that because we are followers of Christ, because we live in the developed world, because we try hard and are good people, we are exempt from adversity, but that is not the teaching of the Bible. In the same way that the Congolese staff could identify with the horrors depicted in *Pushing the Elephant,* we should not be surprised when we also experience hardship. But God does not leave us alone, and we can find strength in sharing both our struggles and our triumphs with those people God has placed around us. None of us can move an elephant on our own. But if we push together, we just might be able to do it!

—RENEÉ

"FOR UNTO US A CHILD IS BORN"

CHILDREN ARE A BLESSING FROM THE LORD.

For you created my inmost being;
you knit me together in my mother's womb.
I praise you because I am fearfully and
wonderfully made.

PSALM 139:13–14

HUMAN RIGHTS ATTORNEY AND AUTHOR John Whitehead once
said: "Children are the living messages we send to a time we will not
see." That truth has become even more real for Reneé and me since
becoming grandparents. Children truly are a gift from God, and babies,
in fact, have a prominent place in the sweep of Scripture. Isaac was the
child of God's promise to Abraham and Sarah. Baby Moses, set adrift in
the bulrushes, grew up in the house of Pharaoh and, as a man, led Israel
out of her captivity and into the Promised Land. Samuel became the
answer to Hannah's prayer and was chosen by God to anoint David, Israel's greatest king. And of course the angel in Bethlehem announced the
arrival of another Baby:

Do not be afraid. I bring you good news that will cause great joy for all the people. Today in the town of David a Savior has been born to you; he is the Messiah, the Lord. This will be a sign to you: You will find a baby wrapped in cloths and lying in a manger. (Luke 2:10—12)

Each of these mothers in the Bible rejoiced at the birth of their children, expecting that God would use them for His great purposes.

But not all mothers rejoice. Poverty can rob mothers and children of their joy. On a trip to Armenia some years ago, I met mothers desperately trying to care for their babies. One lived in a cement house with no glass in the windows. The frigid Armenian winter had driven her and her children to tear up their wooden floor and burn it to keep warm. Another woman dug up old graves to find gold teeth and jewelry so she could

The depth of Armenia's poverty is evident in the lives of Gohar and her family. They live in a ten-by-twenty-four-foot container with two other families, without plumbing or electricity.

feed her family. But worse than that, one young mother—poor, single, desperate for food, and fearing that she could not care for her baby—tried to sell him at the market for $50. She would not even give her baby a name. But a medical worker, hoping that it would help her to bond with the child and keep him, convinced her to name the boy. She named him Edouard, and after trying to sell him for two weeks, she decided to keep this little gift from God.

A little Bolivian girl, "fearfully and wonderfully made" (Psalm 139:14).

More than two billion children live in our world today, each "fearfully and wonderfully made," and "carefully knit ... together" in their mother's womb. But fully half of them are born into the kind of poverty that robs their mothers of joy and stifles their God-given potential. Which of these precious children are tomorrow's Davids or Samuels? How many are Beethovens, Shakespeares, Edisons, and Lincolns? Which ones will become the leaders, scientists, teachers, mothers, and fathers who will shape our world tomorrow? God calls us to protect these little ones. They are His gift to us, "living messages . . . to a time we will not see."

—RICH

TOO MANY CHOICES

WE HAVE A CHOICE ABOUT THE KIND OF ATTITUDE WE BRING TO EACH DAY.

Choose for yourselves this day whom you will serve . . .
but as for me and my household, we will serve the LORD.

JOSHUA 24:15

WHEN MY CHILDREN were young, I agonized over the breakfast cereals they ate, the nursery school they attended, the pediatrician we saw. In many ways, I had too many choices. There are some places in the world, however, where parents have few choices and none of them are good.

If you watched any television back in 1989, you probably remember the images of hollow-eyed children languishing in Romanian orphanages, the legacy of three decades under the leadership of Nicolae Ceausescu. With the fall of communism in that country came the discovery that thousands of children had been warehoused, abandoned, and uncared for in a system of government-run Placement Centers.

Ten years later, as I stood in an eight-by-ten foot cinder block box that was home to a grandmother, three teenage girls, and two toddlers, it was difficult to see how things had improved. But then the family began to tell their story. Toddlers Monica and Cosmine had been among the more than one-hundred-thousand children institutionalized at birth.

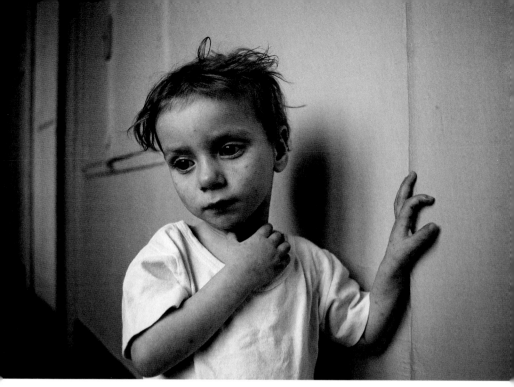

A young Romanian child in an orphanage in 1991.

Like many of the children in Romanian orphanages, they weren't actually orphans. They were the children of young mothers convinced by the state that the best thing a poor family could do was to allow their children to be raised in an institution. Wanting their daughters to have a better life than theirs, Monica's and Cosmine's mothers surrendered their children to the state. What they didn't know was that in the institution, their children would, at best, languish for lack of love and care, and, at worst, be subject to terrible abuse. But desperately poor, these young mothers didn't think they had a choice.

When I consider all the things I have to be thankful for, I rarely consider the luxury of having choices—about the way I spend money, how I use my time, the friends with whom I associate. I make other choices as well, some of which I am even less aware. I have the choice to be affirming rather than critical, to be pleasant rather than unkind, to be generous rather than to keep things for myself. I have a choice about the attitude I bring to each day, each moment, each opportunity that God places before me. And I need to be more intentional about making that choice.

A social worker helped Monica's and Cosmine's mothers understand that they also had a choice to make, and with her help and support, they chose to bring their little ones back home. And when a day care center opened in their neighborhood, Monica and Cosmine were among the very first children to be registered. Their mothers had a second chance to make the right choices for their families. And in the same way that they want their choices to reflect the love that they have for their children, I want my choices to reflect my love for the Savior.

—RENEÉ

A church in Albania chooses to welcome little children.

ETHIOPIA

MYSTERIOUS WAYS

WE NEVER KNOW HOW GOD WILL USE OUR SMALL ACTS OF LOVE FOR HIS GREAT PURPOSES.

God's purpose in all this was to use the church to display his wisdom in its rich variety to all the unseen rulers and authorities in the heavenly places. This was his eternal plan, which he carried out through Christ Jesus our Lord. Because of Christ and our faith in him, we can now come boldly and confidently into God's presence.

EPHESIANS 3:10–12 NLT

"I WAS PRAYING IN THE ROOM. I was naked in the night. Alone. I was going to leave town. I was planning to commit suicide by taking poison." Lying on the floor of her mud-brick home in Ethiopia, the rain pouring through her thatch roof, Wosene was hopeless. "We had nothing to eat and no clothes," she told me.

Wosene had nothing to give her three children, each of whom—instead of attending school—tended cows and was paid in food rather than money. In desperation she cried out to God. "I knelt down and prayed to the Lord, 'Please deliver me,'" Wosene told me. And God did. When she and I spoke, Wosene's life had been transformed. She had a gentle spirit and a joyful, welcoming smile. And she was very pleased that her family now lived in a solid, cement home, her children were in school, and she now had a job that enabled her to support her family.

Yes, God had worked in His mysterious way. Through a grandmother living in a small Nevada town, God answered Wosene's prayers far beyond her imagining. Her life had completely changed when a total stranger named Donna made a commitment to sponsor Wosene's daughter, Sanyat, at a Women of Faith conference. That was the beginning of a big transformation in the lives of both women. Through World Vision, Donna would eventually sponsor Wosene's other children, enable Wosene to move into a sturdier house, and help provide electricity to their home so the children could study at night.

As we sat in Wosene's new home, I asked if her sponsor had written her any letters. Wosene smiled, stood up, walked to a small locked cupboard, and took a key from around her neck. She unlocked the door, carefully lifted out a large plastic bag filled with hundreds of cards and letters, and spread them all out on the table. "These have all come from my sponsor."

Here were hundreds of handwritten cards and letters, each one encouraging this young mother, offering her support and affirmation, and telling her that God loved her dearly. Through those letters Donna had poured her love into this young mother's life. As I saw how Wosene treasured her letters, it was clear that Wosene loved this woman she had never met. I jotted down her name—Donna Galli—and made a note to find her back in the States.

In her desperation, Wosene had come "boldly and confidently into God's presence," pleading for deliverance from her spirit-breaking circumstances. God's answer had come through a grandmother in Nevada who felt God's simple call to sponsor a child.

Wosene's story is not only of a woman who cried out to God. It is also the story of God's mysterious ways: He worked through one of His people half a world away to answer Wosene's prayers and show her and her little family His great love.

We never know how God will use our small acts of love for His great purpose.

—RICH

Wosene stands in the doorway of her old home in Ethiopia.

A MISSIONARY
FROM MY HOME

**GOD CALLS US TO LOVE ONE ANOTHER AND TO
DEMONSTRATE THAT LOVE IN TANGIBLE WAYS.**

*Whoever does not love their brother and sister, whom
they have seen, cannot love God, whom they have not
seen. And he has given us this command: Anyone who
loves God must also love their brother and sister.*

1 JOHN 4:20–21

LET ME NOW INTRODUCE YOU to this amazing grandmother from
Nevada whom God used to bless Wosene and answer the desperate cries
she prayed from her village in Ethiopia.

Donna Galli had been at a Women of Faith conference when an appeal
was made to consider sponsoring a child. "The Lord touched my heart
saying, 'Donna, you have an appointment with a child.'" She looked at
photos of the children who needed a sponsor and was drawn to the heart-
breakingly cold and hopeless eyes of a little girl named Sanyat.

I can do this, Donna thought. *I can help this little child make sure she
has clean water and food in her stomach.*

Wosene treasures all the letters she has received from Donna Galli, her children's sponsor.

But as Donna learned more about Wosene and her children, she realized that she needed to do more. "I was the single mother of three children for a long time, and I clearly remembered the struggles I had. So I thought the least I can do is let her know that she is valuable and that God loves her." And so, since Donna could never afford to go to Ethiopia in person, she began writing letters. "I felt like the Lord told me at that time that I needed to do the best possible job I could. Not halfway. So I felt like I needed to make an emotional connection with Wosene, not just help her physically, and let her know I was praying for her and that I loved her."

After meeting Donna, we invited her to be a special guest at the 2009 Women of Faith conference in Dallas. She was called onto the stage and asked to say a few words about how sponsoring a child a few years earlier had not only changed the life of a family in Ethiopia, but hers as well. And then we surprised her. "Donna, how would you like to go and meet Wosene and her girls in Ethiopia?" She was moved to tears. That next year we filmed Donna's emotional meeting with Wosene and showed it at every Women of Faith conference the following year.

This is how Donna described her meeting: "This is what Wosene said to me when she invited me to her home, 'I had no future, I had no hope. I was dirty, and my children were dirty. Look at my home: it's clean. Look at my face: it's clean. My children are clean. We have hope, and we have a future. We have that because of what Jesus Christ has done through World Vision and because of your love for my family.'"

After Donna saw how God had used her in Wosene's life, she said, "God enabled me to be a missionary from my own home." In 1 John we read, "Whoever does not love their brother and sister, whom they have seen, cannot love God, whom they have not seen." From the other side of the world, Donna took love to the next level with a sister she had never met.

—Rich

Wosene's move from her old hut to her new home reflects a deeper change in her life.

KARI AND THE
SISTERHOOD OF THE
TRAVELING PANTS

**GOD IS ALWAYS WITH US, AND HIS STRENGTH IS
SUFFICIENT TO SEE US THROUGH.**

*Be joyful always; pray continually; give thanks in all
circumstances, for this is God's will for you in Christ Jesus.*

I THESSALONIANS 5:16–18

WE WERE CONNECTING THROUGH PARIS and traveling together
into Niger on one of only two weekly flights into the capital of Niamey.
For me, the close connection wasn't a problem since I only had a carry-
on, but Kari's and Lisa's luggage, which held all their clothing and camera
equipment, was lost.

We scavenged about Niamey for the essentials: tripods, lenses, things
that were absolutely necessary if Kari and Lisa were to take home images
of what the famine was doing to the people of Niger. A local TV station was
kind enough to lend us much of what we needed. But when it came to clothing, Kari and I decided we could just share what I had in my suitcase. So the
journey of the traveling pants began. Back and forth we alternated wearing

Women draw water from a well in Niger.

a not particularly attractive pair of blue capris. Even today we laugh at our efforts to make do with so little of what we ordinarily think we need.

Throughout our time in famine-stricken Niger, we marveled at how so many people were making do. One young mother told of how, when the drought first began, it had taken her just a few minutes to gather leaves to supplement her failing crops. Four months later, it took her an entire day to find enough for just one meal. But at least her two little boys hadn't succumbed to the illnesses to which chronically malnourished children in Niger are most vulnerable—diarrhea, pneumonia, malaria, cholera, and measles. And for this she was thankful. In the face of overwhelming difficulties, she found reason to be grateful.

In spite of their struggles, the apostle Paul told the believers in Thessalonica to approach their everyday lives with prayer and a spirit of joyfulness and thanksgiving, not just when things were going well, but at all times. Paul's advice wasn't "Be thankful *for* your circumstances," but rather "Be thankful *in* your circumstances." In other words, wherever you find yourselves right now, give thanks.

Give thanks no matter what you're going through, no matter how hard your life might be right now. Really? Is that even possible? Paul told us that the secret to having an attitude of gratitude is learning to be content. "I have learned the secret of being content in any and every situation, whether well fed or hungry, whether living in plenty or in want. I can do all this through him who gives me strength" (Philippians 4:12–13).

But contentment isn't the same as resignation, that fatalistic acceptance of the way things are. Rather, contentment comes from the assurance that we are not alone, that no matter how difficult our lives, God is with us, and His strength is sufficient to see us through. Like Paul, we can do all things through Him who gives us the strength to face whatever situation that comes our way—and strength to spare to reach out to those who, like the poor and hungry in Niger, have so little.

—RENEÉ

In Niger, and many places around the world, people make do with almost nothing.

"WE REFUSE TO BE ENEMIES"

Even in the midst of real conflict, God offers a way of peace.

Do not repay anyone evil for evil. Be careful to do what is
right in the eyes of everyone. If it is possible, as far as it
depends on you, live at peace with everyone.

Romans 12:17–18

RENEÉ AND I HAD DINNER IN A CAVE. And it was in that cave where we discovered the life-giving power of peace.

Reneé and I plus a dozen or so American pastors climbed over barricades, sidestepped razor wire, and walked about a mile uphill to reach the cave where Daoud Nassar, a Palestinian Christian living in the West Bank just six miles from Bethlehem, welcomed us to dinner. As we entered, it was hard to miss the large sign that read "We Refuse to Be Enemies."

Daoud and his family had lived on this hundred-acre hillside plot of land for generations. But in 1991 the Israeli government began its attempt to confiscate the family's land in order to build Israeli settlements deemed illegal by the United Nations. The Nassar family resisted peacefully, but since 1991 they have been fighting a courageous and expensive battle in the Israeli courts to keep their land. In the process, Israel has barricaded the road to the Nassar property, forbidden any buildings on the land, and cut off all water and electrical power to the property. The fifty thousand Israeli settlers who now surround them have violently attacked them more than once and burned down many of their olive trees. So now the Nassars live in caves instead of buildings, and they get electrical power from solar panels.

But what is most remarkable about Daoud and his family is their determination to not react with hatred or violence. They really do "refuse to be enemies," and they believe that Muslims, Jews, and Christians can live on the land in peace. Daoud explained: "You cannot overcome the evil with evil. We learned from Jesus Christ to overcome the evil with good. So we cannot handle the situation with hatred but with love. We cannot

Looking toward Jerusalem, where Daoud and others believe that Muslims, Jews, and Christians can live in peace.

Graffiti near the garden of Gethsemane, Jerusalem.

think that with darkness we can achieve light; no, we will only achieve more darkness. But with light we can overcome the darkness."

Few of us will ever face the trials and tribulations that Daoud and his family have faced, but we all face daily decisions about how to respond to those who offend us, take advantage of us, or maybe even deceive us. We can get angry and choose to fight back, try to hurt them, or even initiate a cold war of spite. But the result will inevitably be more anger and more spite. Or we can choose the way of peace.

There are times when Reneé and I hurt one another and say things we regret. At times there doesn't seem to be a way out of the quarrel. But when one of us hugs the other, refusing to be enemies, the coldness thaws and forgiveness wins out.

"Sometimes we fall down," said Daoud. "But we learned how to stand up again like Jesus. He went to the suffering of the cross. But the cross was not the end. It was the path into new life."

—Rich

THE VOICE OF
AN ANGEL

DON'T LET YOUR CIRCUMSTANCES DEFINE YOU!

*Since, then, you have been raised with Christ, set your
hearts on things above, where Christ is seated at the
right hand of God. Set your minds on things above, not on
earthly things. For you died, and your life is now hidden
with Christ in God. When Christ, who is your life, appears,
then you also will appear with him in glory.*

COLOSSIANS 3:1–4

WHEN I JOINED A SORORITY in college, I was assigned a "big sister."
One of Peggy's responsibilities was to share an inspirational saying that
would remind me what was important about being a sorority sister. So at
my initiation ceremony, she presented me with a piece of paper on which
Colossians 3:1–4 was inscribed. Other new members received excerpts
from presidential speeches, witty remarks from celebrities, or inspirational thoughts from the likes of Eleanor Roosevelt, but I received life-
giving wisdom from the apostle Paul, the essence of which was: Don't
let the values and messages of this present world define you; don't allow

the culture in which you're immersed to distract you. No matter what is happening around you, keep your eyes on Jesus. Orient your heart and mind toward Him who died for you. So many times during the course of my college career, I was grateful that I had committed these verses to memory.

Quiquijana, a Quechua village high in the Andes Mountains of Peru, is a long way from my old sorority house. But it was there that I met a little girl who, for me, captured the essence of Paul's message to the Colossians. Part of the welcoming committee, seven-year-old Luz Marina brought me flowers and held my hand. But as others toured the village, we stopped so that she could sing a song. A fire in her home had left her face badly disfigured, she walked with a limp, and she couldn't raise her arm above her head because of scar tissue. But when she opened her mouth to sing, Luz Marina was transformed; her physical limitations seemed to disappear. She was no longer a burn victim, a scarred child with a limp. As if she simply put aside the injuries that could otherwise have defined her, her mind and her heart seemed to transcend her small, broken body as she sang.

Each one of us is uniquely made by God, but circumstances sometimes conspire to make us feel less than what God intended. It is then that we most need Paul's reminder to keep our hearts and minds focused on the truth that is key to our identity: as followers of Christ, we have been raised with Him, and as we turn our hearts and minds heavenward, those earthly things that seek to define us—the situation we find ourselves in, the values and opinions of others—lose their power.

In 1922, Helen Lemmel wrote one of my favorite hymns. The chorus begins, *Turn your eyes upon Jesus, / Look full in His wonderful face. / And the things of earth will grow strangely dim, / In the light of His glory and grace.* If only for a moment, singing enabled Rosemarina to rise above her circumstances. How much more should the knowledge that our lives are "hidden with Christ in God" enable us to rise above our circumstances and let God's love define us.

—RENEÉ

Yashima Janina, eight, holds a bouquet of flowers grown by her family high in the Andes Mountains in Peru.

YOU'RE WEALTHY!

GOD WANTS US TO SEE OUR MONEY AND POSSESSIONS AS GIFTS FROM HIM TO BE USED UNSELFISHLY IN WAYS THAT ARE PLEASING TO HIM.

"The ground of a certain rich man yielded an abundant harvest. He thought to himself, 'What shall I do? I have no place to store my crops.' Then he said, 'This is what I'll do. I will tear down my barns and build bigger ones, and there I will store my surplus grain. And I'll say to myself, "You have plenty of grain laid up for many years. Take life easy; eat, drink and be merry."'"

JESUS IN LUKE 12:16–19

YOU MAY NOT REALIZE THIS, but you are wealthy! OK, now that you're finished rolling your eyes, let me explain. If your annual income is $13,000 a year, you are in the top 10 percent of the world's wealthiest people. An income of $40,000 makes you wealthier than 99 percent of the world's population.[1] So the question is, what will you do with your wealth?

In Jesus' parable in Luke 12, the rich fool had a very confident answer to that question: he would build bigger barns in order to hoard his excess, and he would use his money to "take life easy" and "eat, drink and be merry."

What might this man's decision look like in today's world? It could be the person who lives lavishly, buying whatever they want to satisfy their every desire and denying themselves nothing. But it might be as innocuous as seeing your money, however much you have, as all yours, to do with as you please, with little thought for how God might want you to use it.

I met a man in Zambia who had his own rags-to-riches story. When he was young, Rodrick was arrested and falsely imprisoned for several years. When he was finally released, he returned to his wife and child only to find them living in poverty. Over the next few years they struggled. With no financial assets, a growing family, only sporadic work, and no health care, they barely survived and tragically lost a child to malaria. But Rodrick and his wife, Beatrice, were hardworking and clever. They qualified for a small loan from World Vision and started a business that soon took off. Within five years, Rodrick and Beatrice had created eleven different small businesses, including a beauty salon, a welding business, a pool parlor, and a movie theater that featured a

Rodrick (left) employs orphans in his eleven businesses as a way to give back to his community in Zambia.

small TV set hooked up to a VCR and satellite dish!

I asked Rodrick the same question I just asked you: what will you do with your wealth? Rodrick's answer was very different from that of the rich fool. Rodrick taught a Sunday school class for forty-one orphans, and twice a month he visited each one of these kids where they lived just to check up on them. And Rodrick has a dream: "If God blesses it, Beatrice and I want to use our money to build a school for the orphans." Wow!

Enock, twelve, is one of Rodrick's favorite orphans. He loves to play on the swings Rodrick built for the children in the village.

God cares not only about what we do with our money, but also how we see our money. Any money we have is a gift from Him, to be used in ways that please Him; any money we have is not ours to do with as we please. God responded harshly to the rich man's choice to hoard money and spend it only on himself: "'You fool! This very night your life will be demanded from you.' . . . This is how it will be with whoever stores up things for themselves but is not rich toward God" (Luke 12:20–21).

So let me ask you again: what will you do with your wealth?

—RICH

---

[1] "How Rich You Are," Giving What You Can, accessed January 10, 2013, http://www.givingwhatyoucan.org/resources/how-rich-you-are.php

JUST SHOW UP!

WHEREVER GOD IS CALLING YOU TO BE, BE ALL THERE!

Serve one another in love.

GALATIANS 5:13

THIS MORNING I RECEIVED AN E-MAIL inviting me to connect with someone on LinkedIn who would like to "add me to her professional network." Complete strangers offer me online advice via their blogs about recipes I need to try and DIY projects I can tackle to save both time and money. Friends feel compelled to tweet status updates hourly, and people at church text prayer requests during the sermon. There's no avoiding the reach of social networking. But writing on someone's Facebook wall hardly seems the stuff of relationships, and the appeal of sharing my deepest thoughts in 140 characters escapes me.

Something important is missing from our electronic communications, and a woman Rich and I met while traveling in South Africa put her finger on it. At an area development project where World Vision is working, we joined staff members in singing hymns. When the music stopped, this woman made a beeline for our daughter Grace. "I'm so glad you're here," she said. "I'm so glad that a young person like you cares enough

A caregiver's mission: comforting the elderly in Armenia.

to be here and see what it's like to live in this community." In a world where, with the click of a mouse, we can connect with almost anybody, anywhere, sometimes it's important to just show up.

That truth was obvious when we entered the home of a woman dying of tuberculosis. She was very weak, but because of the love and care of our staff, she took comfort in knowing she would not die alone. And in an AIDS hospice in Cape Town run by Fish Hoek Baptist Church, we saw members of the congregation demonstrate—simply by their presence—the love and compassion of Jesus Christ.

These people showed up, not because they had special skills or state-of-the-art technology, not because they were smarter than most or more spiritual than others. They showed up because that's what was needed. What the people they ministered to needed most was simply someone's presence:

a listening ear, a shoulder to cry on, a hand to hold. And for that, you don't have to be social media–savvy. You just need a tender heart and a willingness to be available to answer God's call.

Not all of us can drill a well or train a farmer or heal a disease. Most of us will never be asked to do so. But as followers of Jesus Christ, we all are called to serve others, even if only by just being there. Jim Elliot, missionary to the Auca Indians of Ecuador, once said, "Wherever you are, be all there. Live to the hilt every situation you believe to be the will of God." In a social media-driven world, take time to be fully present in your community, in your relationships, in your conversations, wherever it might be that God is calling you to show up.

—RENEÉ

Praying with people impacted by HIV and AIDS in South Africa.

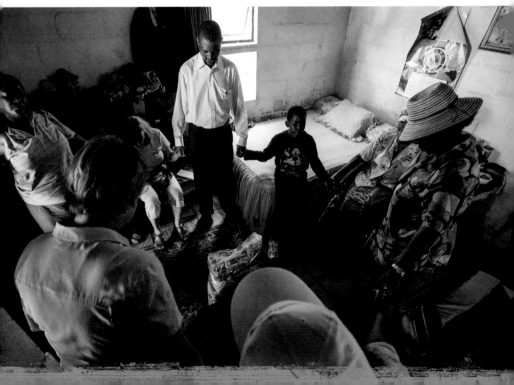

THE TABLES HAVE
BEEN TURNED

WHILE WE MAY NOT UNDERSTAND WHY GOD ALLOWS SUFFERING
IN OUR WORLD, WE ARE NEVERTHELESS COMPELLED TO CARE
FOR THOSE WHOM JESUS DIED TO SAVE.

"Blessed are you who are poor,
for yours is the kingdom of God.
Blessed are you who hunger now,
for you will be satisfied.
Blessed are you who weep now,
for you will laugh."

JESUS IN LUKE 6:20–21

ON THE WALL OF MY OFFICE is a picture of a little boy: Tchafule is from Mozambique, and in my photo he is walking through the bush with a point-ed stick. Not as easy to see is that Tchafule is also carrying home dinner.

When he was eight years old, Tchafule's father died, and Tchafule became the man of the household. He was responsible for providing dinner for his mother and three siblings, and that was usually the family's only meal of the

Three children in Burundi eat their only meal of the day—tiny potatoes harvested too soon.

day. But there were no chickens pecking the ground for wayward kernels of corn, no cattle grazing in a nearby field, no catfish awaiting a fishhook in a stream near his home. So Tchafule traipsed around the countryside near his village hunting. He carried a sharpened stick in his hand, ready to spear the first rat he saw. Rat meat was the family's mainstay. Tchafule's shocking poverty was the senseless kind, the stupid kind. It was the extreme, heart-breaking poverty that need not exist.

After more than a decade of meeting the poorest of the poor, I have no easy explanation for the paradox of God's love on the one hand and such poverty and extreme human suffering on the other. I can offer no trite sayings to rationalize the contradiction away. I feel tension as I hold the Tchafules of this world in one hand and the loving God I know in the other. But when I wrestle with this conflict, I am always taken back to Jesus—God in human form—who, mysteriously, was willing to suffer alongside us. It was this same Jesus who invites the Tchafules of this world—the poor, the hungry, the meek, those who mourn—into His Father's heavenly kingdom.

A child plants corn in South Sudan in the midst of a famine.

Jesus' profound declaration turned the ancient world on its head. His statement was the great equalizer that reset the world's scales of value, worth, and significance. No longer would the powerful, the highborn, the wealthy, and the well-connected be lifted up while the poor and broken were pushed down. Jesus' teaching, this "turning of the tables" has profoundly influenced every human rights movement in the last two thousand years—from the Magna Carta to the American Revolution to the abolition of slavery, civil rights, and the end of apartheid. Jesus changed the course of history when He invited Tchafule and his lot to sit at the head table at the banquet of the King.

Now, a few years later, Tchafule and his family are in a better place. We were able to help his entire community in basic ways. There is a water well nearby as well as goats and chickens for milk and food. Tchafule and his sisters now go to school. I still can't explain the mystery of human suffering, but I do know that Jesus declared Tchafule precious beyond measure and then went to the cross to die for him. And because I love Jesus, I must surely love Tchafule too. It's that simple.

—RICH

SINGING THE WRONG SONG

*Trust in the LORD with all your heart
and lean not on your own understanding;
in all your ways acknowledge him,
and he will make your paths straight.*

PROVERBS 3:5–6

WHENEVER I FACE a situation that seems hopeless or overwhelming, it helps to picture my husband driving to work in the morning, radio tuned to the oldies station. He just loves to sing along with songs he first heard as a teenager, but more often than not, he has trouble with the lyrics. In fact, most of the time, his version doesn't even come close to the actual words.

Conjuring up that image of Rich reminds me to stop and ask myself if things are really as bleak as they seem or am I just feeling that way because, metaphorically, at least, I'm singing the wrong words or maybe even the wrong song. Instead of singing, as my pastor has suggested, *My hope is built on nothing less / Than Jesus' blood and righteousness*, I resort to filling in the blanks with words of my own. My hope is built on nothing less than

Children play near Lake Victoria in Kenya, a community ravaged by AIDS.

Young women support one another at the World Vision Trauma Recovery Center in Phnom Penh, Cambodia.

. . . my money, my connections, my own ability to fix things. Or instead of humming "All Hail the Power of Jesus' Name," I sing the old Frank Sinatra hit "I Did It My Way."

In times of distress, all of us can be tempted to put our confidence in ourselves rather than in God. We place our trust in our own resources rather than in the sovereign care of our heavenly Father. Maybe that's why it so often seems that people who live with very little have greater hope and confidence in the power of God than those whose lives are characterized by material abundance. The poor have no other resources, nothing else in which to put their confidence but God. He is all they have, and they have found—time and again—that He proves Himself to be all they need. Just ask the young women at the World Vision Trauma Recovery Center in Phnom Penh. Rescued from the sex trade, these girls are now back in school studying mathematics and computer science and English. They are learning new skills like weaving, sewing, and hairdressing. They have plans for the future and steadfast hope in a God who has demonstrated His love and care for them by setting them free from a life of misery and despair.

All of us face things in our lives that can leave us feeling hopeless and overwhelmed: the onset of illness, a downturn in the economy, loss of a loved one, abandonment by a spouse. King David faced an advancing army, but rather than give up hope, he put his trust in his heavenly Father. "Some trust in chariots and some in horses, but we trust in the name of the Lord our God. They are brought to their knees and fall, but we rise up and stand firm" (Psalm 20:7–8). Like David, we too can rise up and stand firm in the promises of God and in His mighty power.

—Reneé

WRITING YOUR OWN OBITUARY

WE DON'T GET TO WRITE OUR OWN OBITUARY, BUT WE DO GET TO LIVE THE LIFE THAT WILL BE WRITTEN ABOUT.

Whoever heard me spoke well of me,
and those who saw me commended me,
because I rescued the poor who cried for help,
and the fatherless who had none to assist them.
The one who was dying blessed me;
I made the widow's heart sing.

JOB 29:11–13

HERE IS THE BAD NEWS: everyone reading this book is going to die. In fact, birth and death are the only truly universal human experiences, and the significance of our life lies in what happens in between those two events. So I want to ask you for just a few minutes to think about your own death and to imagine reading your own obituary in the local paper. What would you want it to say about you? Better still, if you could write it yourself, what would you write? How do you want to be remembered?

A Kenyan child who lost her parents to AIDS participates in a program where local families take in orphans.

Would you write about the money you made, the jobs you held, or the real estate you owned? Would you focus on how much time you spent at the office, the way you decorated your home, or the vacations you took? Or would you instead choose to write about the lasting things, the deeper things, the sacred things in your life: the people you loved, the lives you enriched, the ways you helped others, the things you did in obedience to the Lord?

I recently went back and read the obituary of my dear friend Dr. Ted Engstrom, who died in 2006 at the age of ninety. Ted, one of World Vision's pioneers, had become almost a legend for his kindness, faithfulness, and decades of faithful service to the cause of Christ. His influence was felt in many spheres of Christian ministry, including evangelism, education, camps, leadership, and management, and the Christian publishing industry (he wrote more than fifty books in his spare time). He was a friend and counselor to virtually every evangelical leader in America from 1940 until his death. As I read Ted's obituary, a picture of an amazing servant of Christ emerged from his legacy of faithfulness to God, his lifetime of humble and productive service, and the many glowing tributes others who knew and loved him. What a life!

One of my favorite passages in Scripture is actually a kind of obituary. It's found in Job 29:11–17. This man of God had gone through a severe time of testing during which he lost everything—his health, his wealth, his livestock, even his family—yet he still remained faithful to God. In this passage Job was looking back on his life and reminding God of his faithfulness. In a sense, Job was writing his own obituary. Even though he had been a very wealthy man with extensive

A funeral parlor sign in AIDS-ravaged Malawi. What will you be known for when you die?

property, many valuable assets, and quite a résumé of accomplishments, these were not the things he valued most. Instead Job valued his obedience to God, his commitment to justice, his compassion toward the poor, and the things he had done to love his neighbors. Who of us wouldn't want these same words of Job etched on our tombstone? We don't get to write our own obituary, but we do get to live the life that will be written about. And here's some good news: We are God's workmanship, created in Christ Jesus to do good works, which God prepared in advance for us to do.

—RICH

BRAZIL

A COFFIN OF
HIS OWN

EVEN IN THE MIDST OF DIFFICULT TIMES, WE ARE NOT ALONE.

Even though I walk
through the valley of the shadow of death,
I will fear no evil,
for you are with me.

PSALM 23:4 ESV

WE RECENTLY LOST a dear friend. He had been in ill health for some time, but still, his passing took us by surprise. Yet, because he was a man who loved the Lord, there was great rejoicing among his family and friends when we celebrated both the life he lived here on earth and the new life he now lives with his Savior in heaven.

However, in most of the places I visit around the world, there is little celebration when someone dies. More often than not, the victim is a child snatched from life too young. In fact, almost nineteen thousand children will die somewhere in the world today, and the saddest part is that these deaths didn't have to happen. These children suffer from diseases that have been eradicated in the developed world, illnesses brought on by drinking

In Honduras, a community leads a sad procession as it buries one of its smallest members, eight-month-old Alex.

contaminated water, and starvation caused by the poor management of resources. Most of these nineteen thousand deaths were preventable.

When we think of places in the world where children die of preventable causes, we don't usually think of countries like Brazil, host of the 2016 Summer Olympics. Brazil is relatively prosperous, the third largest agricultural producer in the world. But like many other nations, the United States among them, deep pockets of poverty exist alongside areas of affluence. It was into one of these deep pockets that we descended, and it was there that I met Rogerio, a little boy with his very own coffin.

Rogerio was literally starving to death. A picture of his emaciated body and the coffin his father had built to bury him appeared in a local newspaper. And it was that picture which served as a wake-up call to government officials who, with the help of World Vision, began providing food assistance in the northeastern region of the country so that parents like Rogerio's could feed their families.

On the day I met him, Rogerio was running and playing like any other healthy, happy little boy. He bore no evidence of his brush with death except that his father still kept the newspaper clipping and the coffin. At first I thought that was a bit morbid. Why keep such ghastly reminders of that terrible time? And yet what a tangible sign of God's provision for this child!

It occurs to me that I could also use a reminder now and again of all the ways God has come to my rescue, all the times He has held my hand to keep me from falling, even when I have not been aware of my need for His help. More than once, He has walked with me through the valley of the shadow of death—through cancer, the loss of a loved one, the illness of a child—and I have emerged unharmed. Thank You, Father, for Your presence in my life. Help me to remember that You are always with me so that I will not give way to fear!

—RENEÉ

During a famine in southern Sudan, a feeding center is this father's last hope.

PLAYING THE CARDS
YOU WERE DEALT

No one is excused from joining God's great mission in the world, and everyone can make a difference.

As Jesus looked up, he saw the rich putting their gifts into the temple treasury. He also saw a poor widow put in two very small copper coins. "Truly I tell you," he said, "this poor widow has put in more than all the others. All these people gave their gifts out of their wealth; but she out of her poverty put in all she had to live on."

LUKE 21:1–4

HAVE YOU FALLEN INTO THE TRAP of believing that missionary work is best left to professional missionaries? Have you come to believe that Jesus' commands to build the kingdom of God and make disciples of all nations (Matthew 28:19) don't actually apply to every Christian? Surely some people must be excluded. Maybe they aren't spiritual enough, rich enough, or skilled enough to make much of a difference. And haven't some people just been dealt such a bad hand of cards in life that they really can't be expected to serve? Surely they can be excused.

Meet Aurea.

Rescued and taken to the Children of War Center in Gulu, Uganda, a former child soldier bears the scars of war.

My good friend Dr. Steve Hayner was traveling with his daughter when he met Aurea a few years back. Aurea was dealt a hand few of us could bear. In 1994 Aurea was a young wife living with her husband and fifty-three members of her extended family in southern Rwanda. That was the year when the "gates of hell" broke loose, and the horrific Rwandan genocide ravaged the entire nation. Eight hundred thousand people were killed in just one hundred days. Aurea watched in horror as her husband and the other fifty-three members of her family—men, women, and children—were killed right before her eyes. They were shot or hacked to death with machetes. But Aurea, because she was beautiful, was first gang raped and then mutilated and left to die. But she lived.

In addition to her scars, she received two other things that day—the HIV virus and a baby she named Eric, both the result of her rape. Eric too is HIV positive. She and Eric now have a small three-room mud-brick home, about ten feet by twenty. She has found work digging and hoeing a neighbor's fields in exchange for a little food.

Steve's daughter dared to ask Aurea just how she could survive such a devastating and traumatic experience. Aurea reflected and began by saying that she doesn't know how long the two of them will be able to live with the disease they share, but then she said this: "Life is good, because we are in God's hands." Aurea has forgiven the men who raped her and killed her family because "that was what Jesus did for me on the cross."

You would think that Aurea cannot be expected to offer what's left of her life in service to God. She has been through so much! If anyone is excused, surely she is. And besides, what of significance would she have to offer? But you would be mistaken. Aurea has taken an orphan into her home and become a caregiver in her community, visiting those sick with full-blown AIDS. Aurea cares, loves, encourages, comforts, and prays with those God has put in her care. Despite—or maybe because of—the cards she was dealt, Aurea is one of God's most powerful warriors in the great mission to establish His kingdom by demonstrating His love. Consider the cards you have been dealt. Are you playing them for the Lord's glory?

—RICH

PLEASE, WON'T YOU BE MY NEIGHBOR?

CHRIST HAS CALLED US TO EXPAND OUR NEIGHBORHOODS.

"Teacher," [the expert in the law] asked,
"what must I do to inherit eternal life?"

"What is written in the Law?" [Jesus] replied.
"How do you read it?"

He answered, "'Love the Lord your God with all your heart
and with all your soul and with all your strength and with
all your mind'; and, 'Love your neighbor as yourself.'"

"You have answered correctly," Jesus replied.
"Do this and you will live."

LUKE 10:25–28

AS THE MOTHER OF FIVE CHILDREN, I've seen my share of soccer games, and I know that while the outcome of the game is often in doubt, what takes place at halftime never is. Any self-respecting soccer mom knows that passing out snacks is often the highlight of the game, especially

Halftime at a soccer game becomes a chance to educate peers on HIV and AIDS in Malawi.

if your team is not playing well. So I was surprised when halftime was called at a soccer game in Senzani, Malawi, and there was not a single snack in sight. Instead, players presented songs, dances, and dramatic vignettes on the topic of HIV and AIDS.

A young woman who was HIV positive gave a speech, a group of adolescent boys acted out a skit about the transmission of AIDS, and a talented group of teenagers sang several songs about keeping oneself pure. All were part of a community effort to break the stigma of AIDS, to get it out in the open so that people had a fighting chance against this terrible disease.

Looking back, none of this seems so unusual now, but in 2003, talking openly about HIV and AIDS was unheard of. The stigma attached to the disease had forced a generation into silence. One pastor we met had performed five funerals in one day for people from his congregation who had died of AIDS, but he had never once spoken of the disease from the pulpit.

Not all fun and games, soccer players in Senzani, Malawi, use their matches to educate and break the stigma of AIDS.

For too many years, HIV and AIDS were considered diseases that only struck people who engaged in risky behaviors and, that, those infected deserved whatever happened to them. People drew the same conclusion about AIDS sufferers as did the priest and the Levite about the man lying beaten on the side of the road in Jesus' parable of the good Samaritan. When the religious leaders came upon him, they crossed over to the other side. They didn't know who he was, where he came from, or even what had caused his terrible situation. In fact, as Jesus told the story, the only clues we have are that the victim was naked, so there's no way to tell where he's from by his outward appearance, and that he's half-dead, and therefore unable to be identified by his language or dialect.

The priest and the Levite had no way of knowing whether this person lying on the side of the road was an innocent victim or someone who, because of his risky behavior, deserved what had befallen him. And I think that was the very point Jesus was making. In answer to the question "Who is my neighbor?" Jesus wants us to understand that our neighbor isn't limited to the person who lives next door. My neighbor isn't necessarily some-one who dresses like me or speaks my language, who shares my politi-cal convictions or adheres to my religious beliefs. The good Samaritan found his neighbor bleeding on the side of the road. I might find mine in the seat next to me on an airplane or pushing a cart in the grocery store. Who is God calling you to be neighbor to today?

—RENEÉ

"GO AND DO LIKEWISE"

As God's people, we are to help even those we have never met.

"A man was going down from Jerusalem to Jericho, when
he was attacked by robbers. They stripped him of his
clothes, beat him and went away, leaving him half dead.
A priest happened to be going down the same road, and
when he saw the man, he passed by on the other side. So
too, a Levite, when he came to the place and saw him,
passed by on the other side."

JESUS IN LUKE 10:30–32

THE PARABLE OF THE GOOD SAMARITAN is perhaps the most profound moral teaching of all time. Jesus had just stated that the second greatest commandment, after "Love God," is to "Love your neighbor as yourself." That's when He got "pushback" from the legal expert looking for a loophole: "And just exactly who is my neighbor, Jesus?" Jesus answered with this well-known parable.

Now who of us wants to think of ourselves as the priest or Levite who ignored the man and passed by on the other side? Good heavens, we would never be like that! But wait. Have you ever driven by a homeless man standing on the road with his sign and done nothing? Have you changed the channel when a report of some humanitarian tragedy was being aired? Weren't you, then, just like the priest and the Levite, aware of a need and able to help but you passed by without a second look or thought? Who *is* your neighbor?

A few years back I met a Korean man in New York who had once been helped by a good Samaritan. His family had lost everything in the Korean War. When I told him I worked for World Vision, he smiled and told me that charities like World Vision had helped his family in critical ways after the war ended. They had provided him with books and school supplies so he could finish his education. He never knew who the American donors were who gave their money to help, but to this day he has remained grateful.

This "Who Is My Neighbor?" lesson is surely one of the hardest teachings of Jesus because it sets a very high bar: we have responsibility for anyone in need whom we are able to assist. Now let me confess that I, too, have driven by homeless people and not stopped; I too have failed to send a contribution to help in every tragedy. Even Jesus didn't heal every sick person He saw. But a bright thread of love and compassion ran

all through Jesus' life and ministry. He was constantly giving and loving those around Him, and I think He expects to see that same bright thread of compassion woven through our lives. At the end of the story, Jesus asked His lawyer friend which of the three he thought was a good neighbor. The man answered, "The one who had mercy on him." Jesus replied, "Go and do likewise" (v. 37).

We don't know anything about this man who was beaten by robbers and left to die by the side of the road. Was he a Jew or a pagan? Was he himself a thief? And what happened to him after he recovered? I think Jesus' point was that we don't need to know those things; we just need to respond and leave the rest to God.

By the way, I do know what happened to the Korean man whom strangers helped sixty years ago. His name is Ban Ki-moon, and he grew up to become secretary general of the United Nations!

"Go and do likewise."

—RICH

Which one of these boys from India might become another Ban Ki-moon secretary general of the United Nations?

CHILD SOLDIERS

WE ARE SAVED NOT BY OUR OWN MERIT, BUT BY THE BLOOD OF JESUS CHRIST.

When the kindness and love of God our Savior appeared,
he saved us, not because of righteous things we had done,
but because of his mercy. He saved us through the washing
of rebirth and renewal by the Holy Spirit, whom he poured
out on us generously through Jesus Christ our Savior.

TITUS 3:4–6

SOME WORDS JUST AREN'T MEANT to go together. I think *child* and *soldier* are two of them. Tragically, tens of thousands of children are involved in fifteen conflicts taking place somewhere in the world today. Some children participate in actual combat; others are used as spies, land mine sweepers, porters, or even sexual slaves.

While the notion of child soldiers is inconceivable to most of us, there are those who use children in battle because they see them as a source of cheap labor, expendable, easily brainwashed, and therefore willing to commit terrible acts of atrocity at the behest of their commanding officers. For more than two decades the LRA preyed upon children in Northern Uganda, kidnapping and then forcing them to become soldiers.

World Vision's Children of War Center in Northern Uganda provides play therapy for children who escaped from the LRA.

Thomas is a young man who had the misfortune of growing up there, and at an age when most boys should be playing soccer or hanging out with friends, he was taken from his home and forced to murder his own people. As he shared his story with me, his hands began to shake, and I instinctively reached out to hold them. But when he explained that he had been ordered to drench the hands I now held in the blood of his victims, a wave of revulsion swept over me, and I struggled to hang on.

Thomas was too ashamed and afraid to return to his home after what he had done, and his parents had not been to see him since his escape from the LRA. He thought it was because they lived a long way off, but I was told that it was just too difficult for them to receive back into their arms a child they knew had committed such unspeakable horrors.

How difficult indeed, and yet, remarkably, that is just what God has done for each of us. Our heavenly Father has taken our sinful, trembling hands in His and has welcomed us into His family. Like Thomas,

A boy reflects during devotions at the Children of War Center in Northern Uganda.

we come to Him ashamed and afraid, certain that He could never love someone like us. But then God does something incredible, wonderful, unexpected. He "demonstrates his own love for us in this: While we were still sinners, Christ died for us" (Romans 5:8). Because the shed blood of His Son Jesus paid the price for our sins, God accepts us as forgiven and invites us to be His children. So if you're waiting until you get your life in order, waiting until you are good enough to approach the throne of God, you can stop right now. Nothing you could ever do will make you worthy of God's love. But that's OK. God welcomes you as you are. "There is now no condemnation for those who are in Christ Jesus" (Romans 8:1).

—RENEÉ

NOT THE ANSWER
I EXPECTED

GOD SOMETIMES ANSWERS OUR PRAYERS IN WAYS WE WOULD NOT CHOOSE.

"For my thoughts are not your thoughts,
neither are your ways my ways,"
declares the LORD.
"As the heavens are higher than the earth,
so are my ways higher than your ways
and my thoughts than your thoughts."

ISAIAH 55:8–9

YOU COULD SAY that Ray Norman and his family were in the wrong place at the wrong time when the 9/11 attacks occurred. Ray was World Vision's country director in Mauritania, an impoverished Islamic republic in West Africa. Ray had felt called to serve the poor and be an ambassador for Christ in this place. But in Mauritania any form of Christian witness is prohibited and even punishable by death. So Ray and his family prayed that God would find a way for them to demonstrate the love of Christ. But God's answer was not the one Ray had expected or hoped for.

A few weeks after 9/11, Ray and his ten-year-old daughter, Hannah, were in their vehicle when a lone, turbaned man in flowing robes approached their car and began shooting. Ray stepped on the gas but not before the bullets had taken their toll. Ray had been shot through the arm, and when he looked at Hannah, he saw that she was slumped next to him in a pool of blood that was quickly filling her seat. Ray remembers crying out to God. This anguished father, who had offered his life in service to God, cried out in that moment, "Hannah's life was *not* part of the deal!" Little Hannah had been shot in the chest and was urgently airlifted to France for surgery.

After weeks of recovery, prayer, and agonizing over the huge decision of whether to go back, Ray, Hannah, and the rest of the family returned to Mauritania to resume their ministry. Unexpectedly, as soon as they returned, they were engulfed by the love and support of the Muslim community, men and women who loved them and were horrified by what had happened. Ray asked to meet with a leading Muslim leader to discern whether it was wise for World Vision's work in this country to continue. This was the man's reply: "We Muslims give alms and help the poor because we are *instructed* to do so; but with World Vision, you work with the poor *because you love the poor*. This is different. This is what sets you apart. If for no other reason, stay in this country and teach our people how to love their poor." Ray was shocked. This was the answer to his prayer that God would find a way for him to demonstrate the love of Christ. It just wasn't the answer he had expected.

More miracles happened. Hannah wanted to visit the man, now in prison, who had shot her, so that she could tell him she forgave him. The president himself intervened to grant this unorthodox prison visit, and when the day came, Hannah not only forgave her assailant, but her mother, Hélène, read to the man from the Bible—an action that could have gotten her thrown in jail. But instead, so remarkable was the forgiveness of this young girl that it made headlines. All of Mauritania was captivated by this extraordinary story of Christian forgiveness.

So, yes, God bids us to pray, but always with the knowledge that His ways are higher than our ways.

—Rich

A Muslim traditional healer in Niger.

MODERN FAMILY

THROUGH THE DEATH AND RESURRECTION OF JESUS, WE HAVE BEEN ADOPTED INTO GOD'S FAMILY.

Long before he laid down earth's foundations, he had us in mind, had settled on us as the focus of his love, to be made whole and holy by his love. Long, long ago he decided to adopt us into his family through Jesus Christ.

EPHESIANS 1:4–5 MSG

A QUICK LOOK at a newspaper or a blog or even a television sitcom makes it clear that the very idea of family in modern culture is changing. Yet the very special place God gave mothers in His design has not changed, and it is a role that only they can fill.

God has entrusted mothers with the awesome task of building a home. We preside over the shaping of young minds, translate biblical principles into human character, and with much prayer, seek to mold our children into competent, responsible, godly adults. Unfortunately, crumbling social structures and devastating poverty prevent some mothers from doing the job God intended. So He expands the hearts of others who widen their family circle to include little girls like Valentina.

Valentina was born to a mother who gave her up to a Romanian orphanage. Whether it was because of her daughter's cleft palate, or because she felt ill-equipped to handle her medical care, or simply because she believed that Valentina would be better off in a state-run placement center is not clear. What is clear, however, is that had Valentina been left to grow up in an institution, her physical condition would have subjected her to the worst kind of abuse and neglect. But fortunately for this little girl, a World Vision-trained foster mother named Anna rescued her, and when I met Valentina, she was thriving. Because Anna reached out to an abandoned child, that child now knows the joy of a warm embrace, the soothing sounds of a mother's voice, the security of her own home.

It occurs to me that what Anna has done for Valentina illustrates, however imperfectly, what God has done for you and me. He has expanded His family circle to include us who once were far away from Him, and He has brought us near through the blood of His Son, Jesus (Ephesians 2:13). Like abandoned children condemned to live imprisoned in an institution, we were once imprisoned in a life of sin. But thanks be to God! He reached out to us and made us alive with Christ,

This shelter in Romania helps teen mothers care for their babies.

In Romania, babies who would have been abandoned sleep peacefully.

forgiving our sins, canceling the written code which condemned us, and nailing it to the cross (Colossians 2:13–14)! Scripture tells us that even before God gave the earth its form, He had us in mind, and He made a way through the death and resurrection of our Lord Jesus Christ for us to be adopted into His family (Ephesians 1:4–6). As John the apostle proclaimed, "To all who received [Jesus], to those who believed in his name, he gave the right to become children of God" (John 1:12), and that is what we are!

—RENEÉ

IT'S ALL RELATIVE

GOD IS SERIOUS ABOUT HIS COMMAND TO US: WE ARE TO
HELP THE LESS FORTUNATE.

Rescue the perishing;
don't hesitate to step in and help.
If you say, "Hey, that's none of my business,"
will that get you off the hook?
Someone is watching you closely, you know —
Someone not impressed with weak excuses.

PROVERBS 24:11–12 MSG

HAVE YOU HAD A GOOD YEAR? Consider the year that baseball
player Albert Pujols signed a $240 million deal to play for the Los Ange-
les Angels. Or when Mariah Carey was offered $17 million a year to be a
judge on *American Idol.* And Jay Leno had a bad year, offering to cut his
salary from $30 to $15 million so *The Tonight Show* wouldn't have to lay
off so many staff. I guess good or bad is all relative.

But Mary Bwalya, a seventy-something grandmother in Zambia,
clearly had a bad year a few years ago when her son and daughter-in-law
both died, leaving her with four young children to raise. When she learned
of her son's death, this elderly widow traveled several hundred miles by

bus to rescue her four grandchildren, but not before they had almost died from hunger. Then the situation got worse as all five of them fell deeper into poverty.

Thousands of miles away, I was hosting a World Vision donor conference on AIDS in New York. On the final evening, after I challenged each of the donors there to sponsor some children, my wife reminded me that we should respond as well. Despite my protest that we already sponsored a dozen kids, I relented. So that night, I rather reluctantly became the new sponsor for Morgan and Jackson, two brothers, aged ten and thirteen—and Mary Bwalya's grandsons. I didn't know that night that my small decision may have meant the difference between their life and their death.

Two years later, on a trip to Zambia to film for a TV special, I had the opportunity to meet Morgan, Jackson, and their courageous grandmother.

Rich visits Jackson (in red) and his brother, Morgan, in their village in Zambia.

Courageous Mary Bwalya rescued her grandchildren.

As we arrived in the village, Mary Bwalya spotted us and broke into a run. She fell at my feet and grabbed my hands, weeping and saying "thank you" over and over. "When I learned that a family in America had sponsored these two boys, I knew that God was replacing the parents they had lost. Thank you!"

I was stunned that my small decision to pay about two dollars a day to help these boys may have literally saved their lives. Now the boys were prospering: they lived in a new house, and they had books for school and even new Bibles to read. Mary Bwalya and her grandchildren were having a good year.

Just how responsible are we for others? Proverbs 24 tells us that God wants us to "step in and help" those who are struggling and that "he is watching [us] closely" and is "not impressed with weak excuses." And didn't Jesus Himself declare that the second greatest commandment—second only after loving God—is to love our neighbors? And, to be clear, this is a commandment, not a suggestion. You may not have had a year like Albert Pujols, Jay Leno, or Mariah Carey once had, but compared to people like Mary Bwalya, I'll bet you had a pretty good one. I guess it's all relative.

—RICH

HE AIN'T HEAVY,
HE'S MY BROTHER

A BURDEN SHARED IS A BURDEN LIFTED.

*Carry each other's burdens, and in this way you
will fulfill the law of Christ.*

GALATIANS 6:2

AS A MOTHER, my desire has always been that my children would grow
into competent, independent adults, but not at the expense of developing
compassionate, caring hearts for others. In a world that often promotes
individual rights over those of the community, I want to offset that idea
with the biblical message that we have a responsibility for the welfare of
those around us, that we are to love God and to love our neighbors. I saw
that idea beautifully demonstrated in a small nursery school in Malawi.

Shrieks of laughter abruptly turned into quiet anticipation as 120
children in an AIDS-devastated community lined up for a bowl of hot
porridge. For most of them, this was the only meal they had eaten since
the previous morning, and they were hungry. Anastasia, the director of the
day care center, explained that ninety of the children were orphans living
in child-headed households and they would have no other opportunity

THIS PAGE AND NEXT: Children receive a warm meal at Anastasia's day care center in Malawi.

to eat that day. Money was tight, and she could only afford to feed them one meal.

Anastasia wasn't always a day care director, but when her sister died of AIDS and she took on the responsibility of caring for her niece, she decided to include the eighty-nine other children in her community who had also lost their parents to the disease. She was an excellent teacher, and once breakfast was finished, the children showed me what they had learned, reciting in unison the alphabet, numbers, even the months of the year—all in English.

In addition to the few mothers helping at the center, fifteen other local women were working in a nearby field, tending maize. Their goal was to raise enough money selling their crops so the day care center could stay open until 5:00 p.m. instead of closing at 11:30 each morning. Their earnings would also help buy enough food for the children to have a second meal during the school day. The community was pulling together to care for its most vulnerable members—the children—by bearing the burden resulting from the deaths of so many parents.

The community was living out what the apostle Paul identified as a fundamental part of the life of every believer: "Carry each other's burdens, and in this way you will fulfill the law of Christ" (Galatians 6:2). Anastasia and a handful of other women in her community took that message to heart. They assumed responsibility for the child-headed households of Senzani, Malawi, and took upon their own weary shoulders the burdens those ninety orphans otherwise would have carried alone.

As members of God's family, the welfare of others is our concern. Is there a brother or sister whose burden you could help lift today?

—Reneé

BLINDING LIGHT

The darker our darkness, the more brilliant is the good news of our forgiveness in Christ.

"The people living in darkness
have seen a great light;
on those living in the land of the shadow of death
a light has dawned."

From that time on Jesus began to preach, "Repent, for the
kingdom of heaven has come near."

MATTHEW 4:16–17

WHEN RENEÉ AND I WERE IN THE NETHERLANDS, we had the opportunity to visit a labyrinth of caves near the city of Maastricht. During World War II people had sought refuge there. At one point in the tour, our guide turned off all of the lights so we could experience total darkness. It was somewhat terrifying and disorienting to be in a place completely devoid of light. Later, when we emerged, the sunshine seemed blinding by comparison.

Several years ago Northern Uganda might have qualified as the darkest place on earth from a spiritual perspective. The LRA was terrorizing local civilians and kidnapping children to turn them into rebel fighters. Many

Two children watch a therapy session for former child soldiers at the Children of War Center.

boys and girls, at the point of a gun, were forced to brutally kill family members and friends.

In the midst of this dark place, the World Vision rehabilitation center shone a bright light by taking in the broken child soldiers and child brides who had managed to escape Kony's army. We offered a safe place of healing, restoration, and reacclimation to the light for those who had experienced years of living in darkness.

One day Reneé and I had the privilege of witnessing the arrival of two teenage boys who had been rescued from the LRA. The big gates swung open, and a vehicle drove into the compound. Michael and Joseph weren't prepared for what was about to happen to them. Both had spent years with Kony and the LRA, and they had undoubtedly been forced to kill and maim hundreds of their own countrymen. Michael's left arm was withered from a gunshot wound sustained before he was fully grown. And both boys had been poisoned with lies about what would be done to them at the rehabilitation center. Fear was in their lifeless eyes as they entered the camp. They weren't at all prepared for the brilliant light of forgiveness.

Instead of the torture and punishment they had expected, fifty other boys and girls surrounded their car, dancing, clapping, and singing hymns of praise and songs of welcome to these two broken boys. As the two stumbled from the vehicle, smiles, handshakes, and high fives were offered from other damaged children who also knew something about the darkness from which Michael and Joseph had emerged. A spark of life returned to the boys' eyes. The corners of their mouths began to turn up. They were home. The singing crowd spilled directly into the chapel for a spontaneous worship service to welcome them back. And that's when I saw it. I could see the good news—the glorious life-changing gospel and the unthinkable possibility of forgiveness—washing

Children experience love and restorative healing at the Children of War Center in Gulu, Uganda.

over Michael and Joseph like a new dawn. They had realized that they could be made clean again just as Jesus had promised:

> *"He has sent me to proclaim freedom for the prisoners and recovery of sight for the blind, to release the oppressed, to proclaim the year of the Lord's favor."* (Jesus reading from the prophets in Luke 4:18–19)

This blinding truth had pierced their darkness just as it had once pierced mine.

—RICH

HEARTBREAK

GOD CAN ONLY BEGIN TO USE US WHEN OUR HEARTS ARE BROKEN
BY THE THINGS THAT BREAK HIS HEART.

*"I will give you a new heart and put a new spirit in
you; I will remove from you your heart of stone and
give you a heart of flesh."*

EZEKIEL 36:26

WHEN I RETURN FROM TRAVELING TO SEE the work of World
Vision in the field, one of the questions I'm most frequently asked is, "Did
you have fun?" Well-meaning people don't quite know what to say when
I tell them I've just returned from Northern Uganda, or the DRC, or the
West Bank. So, sympathetic to their discomfort, I usually respond with
something like "The people I met were wonderful" or "I learned so much.
Would you like me to tell you about it?" But *fun* . . . ? (Oh, there was that
entertaining ride on Chumpa the elephant!)

For many people, it's difficult to imagine what traveling looks like
without the guidebook, the map, and the resort hotel. I know that when
we go on a family vacation, our goal as tourists is to find comfort, rest,
and relaxation. By contrast, traveling with World Vision is often fraught
with delay and discomfort. But we've discovered that you can't enter
into the lives of the people our staff serves without feeling at least a little

uncomfortable. You can't look into the eyes of a hurting child without, in fact, having your heart broken.

But that's OK, because only at the point in our travels when our hearts are broken does God begin to use us. Bob Pierce, the founder of World Vision, once prayed that God would break his heart with the things that break the heart of God. He didn't want his heart to become so calloused to the pain, the suffering so routine, that he could ignore it. He feared that, somewhere down the line, he might become numb to the things that so touched and troubled him at first, so in the flyleaf of his Bible, he wrote that now-famous prayer.

If, like Bob Pierce, I were to write a prayer for my travels to the difficult places where World Vision works, it might read something like this:

A storm bears down on an already vulnerable refugee camp in Darfur, Sudan.

Six-year-old Geovani and his family in Honduras survived the devastation of Hurricane Mitch in 1998.

Break my cold, hard, self-centered heart, O God, and replace it with a heart that beats as one with Yours. Don't let me be content to be a tourist in this world, just passing through, seeking only to maximize my pleasure and minimize my discomfort. Rather, allow me to be attentive to what You see, aware of the suffering of those You came to save.

Put within me a heart that is tender and responsive to the needs of Your world, a heart that will never again look at the hungry and the homeless, the sick and the dying, and conclude that they are someone else's problem. Give me a heart that will never allow me to consider how little I can get by with but only how much more I can do.

And then, Father, with my eyes fixed upon Jesus and the sure and certain hope of heaven before me, give me a willingness to stop and get my hands dirty in being about Your business helping those in need around me. Amen.

—RENEÉ

WHEN GOD CALLS US TO WAIT

SOMETIMES GOD ANSWERS OUR PRAYERS IN UNEXPECTED WAYS. HE CALLS US TO BE PATIENT, TO ENDURE, AND TO TRUST THAT HIS PLAN FOR OUR LIVES IS BETTER THAN OURS.

We continually ask God to fill you with the knowledge of his will through all the wisdom and understanding that the Spirit gives, so that you may live a life worthy of the Lord and please him in every way: bearing fruit in every good work, growing in the knowledge of God, being strengthened with all power according to his glorious might so that you may have great endurance and patience.

COLOSSIANS 1:9–11

PATIENCE IS NOT ONE OF MY STRONG SUITS. I've never been good at waiting in lines, sitting in traffic jams, or enduring flight delays. But even harder for most of us is being patient with God.

I have met many people who yearn to know God's clear calling on their life. Some of them have a specific passion such as helping the poor, going out as a missionary, or working with at-risk youth. Others hope for a certain kind of career opportunity or yearn to be married and have a family. And when those doors don't seem to open, they become impatient with God. Yet the apostle Paul prayed for the Colossians that they would have endurance and patience.

Ming Chan was impatient with God too. As a child, she survived the Cambodian genocide. When the terrible reign of the Khmer Rouge was over, Ming had only three family members left. As a young woman, she began to take care of her younger brother and sister and her mother. Ming knew that the work of caring for her family meant that she might never realize her dream of being married and having children of her own.

So Ming chose to bloom where she was planted. She decided to do something about the poverty and social problems rampant in postgenocide Cambodia. She started youth clubs that would help children in school, train them about their rights, protect them from trafficking, and teach them to value their parents and themselves. More than six hundred children have gone through her clubs, and they all look up to the woman who invested her life in theirs. The name *Ming* means "Auntie," and it's the nickname the children gave her. "I am not married," Ming told me, "but God has given me a lot of children."

When I met my wife, Reneé, she was just nineteen. Her dream was to become a lawyer and spend her life helping the poor. She did become a lawyer, but then she chose to stay at home to raise our five kids. Twenty-five years went by, and her dream of helping the poor seemed like it would never come to pass . . . until one day God led her crazy husband to serve with World Vision. Now Reneé is helping the poor all over the world. She is my partner in traveling the globe, serving "the least of these," and even writing

Part of Ming Chan's work in Cambodia is empowering children to march for their rights.

After surviving the Khmer Rouge genocide, Ming Chan chose to bloom where she was planted, starting youth clubs.

this book. Sometimes we simply need to be patient because God answers prayers in His timing and His way.

Abraham was one hundred years old when his promised son, Isaac, was born. Joseph was sold as a slave and spent years in prison before becoming the Pharaoh's right-hand man and saving Egypt and Israel from famine. Moses was eighty years old before God called him to lead Israel out of their Egyptian captivity.

God's way is not our way. God always answers prayer. Sometimes He says "Yes," sometimes "No," and sometimes "Wait." Being told to wait is sometimes the hardest but most life-changing and fulfilling answer of all.

—RICH

ANGELA AND FLORENCE

OUR LOVE FOR OUR CHILDREN IS BUT A PALE REFLECTION OF THE FATHER'S LOVE FOR US.

"This son of mine was dead and is alive again; he was lost and is found."

JESUS IN LUKE 15:24

MY DAUGHTER HANNAH recently graduated from law school. This event represented the culmination of years of hard work, bringing her one step closer to her goal of becoming an attorney. But when Hannah and I traveled to Northern Uganda, we met a young woman whose goal of becoming an attorney will never be realized.

Angela was attending boarding school in Northern Uganda when, on October 10, 1996, a rebel group from the LRA abducted 139 students. Negotiations led to the release of all but thirty of the girls; those left were taken as *wives* for rebel commanders. Gone from her mother for nine years before she was able to escape, Angela returned home infected with AIDS, her health and her childhood forever taken away. When we met, twenty-seven-year-old Angela was struggling to finish high school. Gone was her dream of a career in law.

As Hannah and I talked with Angela and her mother, Florence, their story evoked memories of a phone call I'd received two months earlier, the kind of call a mother dreads. It was from a hospital in Washington, DC, informing me that Hannah had been in an accident and had suffered multiple fractures and a possible broken neck. I rushed to the airport and flew to be with her. To my relief and amazement, by the time I arrived, the doctors had inexplicably changed their diagnosis. Despite being struck by a car while walking across the street, Hannah had, in fact, no broken bones.

Sitting across from Florence, I recalled how desperate I had felt. I could hardly imagine what it must have been like for her. My ordeal lasted only the twelve hours it took me to get to Hannah's bedside and see for myself that she was all right. What about Angela's mother? Had she awakened all 3,285 mornings that Angela was gone, wondering if she was still alive, hoping this might be the day her only child finally returned?

After a long nightmare, Florence's dream was realized: her daughter was returned.

Florence holds the hand of a young woman she is counseling.

Like the father in the parable of the lost son, Florence never gave up hope that someday she would be reunited with her precious daughter. Of course the prodigal had chosen to leave of his own accord, but his father still longed for his return in the same way that Florence longed for Angela's, in the same way that God longs for the return of all His lost children. Florence never stopped believing that Angela would come back. Putting her faith in God alone, she entrusted the safety of her daughter to Him who loves her even more than Florence does.

You may not have experienced the physical loss of a loved one as Florence did, but perhaps there is someone in your life who is spiritually lost. Like her, you too can trust your lost son or daughter, husband or wife, to God. Rest, knowing that like the shepherd searching for the lost sheep or the widow looking for the lost coin, God will never stop pursuing the one you love. Great is the rejoicing in heaven every time one lost soul returns to Him!

—Reneé

A FIRM PLACE
TO STAND

> EACH ONE OF US WILL FIND OURSELVES IN A SLIMY PIT FROM
> WHICH WE NEED RESCUE. BUT JESUS OFFERS US HIS HELPING
> HAND AND A FIRM PLACE ON WHICH TO STAND.

He lifted me out of the slimy pit,
out of the mud and mire;
he set my feet on a rock
and gave me a firm place to stand.
He put a new song in my mouth,
a hymn of praise to our God.
Many will see and fear the LORD
and put their trust in him.

PSALM 40:2–3

MAYBE YOU CAN'T TOTALLY RELATE to being rescued from a slimy pit, but a man I met in Ethiopia surely could. "I was a drunkard," Bzuneh told me. "And when I was drunk, I beat my wife. I abused her. Whatever money I made, I spent on beer." Bzuneh fell so low that his wife and children finally left him. He hit the bottom of his slimy pit on the night he stumbled and fell into the gutter, injuring himself badly enough that he

Once drunkards, Bzuneh and his wife, Bilile, now stand tall in their community.

couldn't even climb out. The next morning he was discovered by a good Samaritan who offered help and cared for him until he was better. That experience is what it took for God to get Bzuneh's attention.

Desperate for anything that might turn his life around, Bzuneh went back to church where he found people who were willing to help him. "At church I saw the lives of changed drunkards," he told me. Over time, both Bzuneh and his wife became Christians. Remarkably, Bzuneh testified, "It took me just one week to quit drinking."

With his new faith as a foundation for life, Bzuneh began to change, and so did his family. He worked hard as a farmer, started a fertilizer business, and rebuilt his home. He now speaks lovingly of the wife he once beat: "I want to buy good things for her. I wish good things for her always." And perhaps the greatest evidence of his changed life is that this former town drunk was elected by his peers to be president of the local agricultural co-op and was named "Farmer of the Year." Bzuneh had taken the helping hand of Jesus who lifted him out of the mud and mire, gave him a firm place to stand, and put a new song in his mouth.

We all need a firm place to stand as we face the inevitable challenges and pitfalls of life. And even though most of us don't have lives as desperate as Bzuneh's, all of us do fall into our own slimy pits and need to be rescued. When I first turned to Jesus as a young man, I was in a slimy pit of my own making. Having survived a very dysfunctional home, I had a chip on my shoulder and was arrogant and self-reliant. On the outside I may have looked successful, but I was on a collision course that would have ultimately found me facedown in the mud and mire of my own self-destructive behavior. But Christ gave me a firm place to stand, a place of forgiveness and acceptance, a place of truth and integrity, a place of healing and love. Just as He did for Bzuneh, God put a new song in my mouth.

Whatever pit you might fall into—a pit of broken relationships, bitterness, poor health, addictive behavior, financial stress, family dysfunction, or career disappointment—Jesus is reaching out His hand to you. Grab hold of it and don't let go.

—Rich

NIGHT COMMUTERS

I am always with you;
you hold me by my right hand.
You guide me with your counsel,
and afterward you will take me into glory.
Whom have I in heaven but you?
And earth has nothing I desire besides you.
My flesh and my heart may fail,
but God is the strength of my heart
and my portion forever.

PSALM 73:23–26

MY GRANDSON HATES IT when I try to hold his hand. As quickly as I reach out to grasp his chubby little toddler fingers, he pulls away, seeking the independence that, at his age, can sometimes lead to trouble. How tightly I reassert my grasp depends on where we are. At the park there is nothing better than to watch him run and play on his own, but on a busy street, nothing can dislodge my grip.

I walked beside Lily, a beautiful sixteen-year-old girl, as she held the hands of her little sisters, Harriet and Nancy. They were headed to the

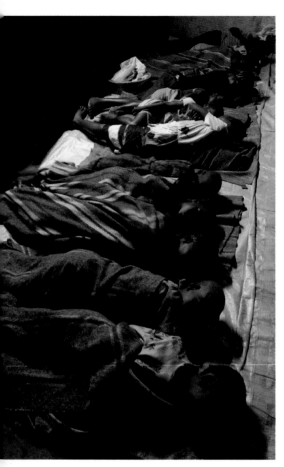
Seeking safety, children cram into centers for night commuters like Noah's Ark.

Noah's Ark Children's Center in the city of Gulu, Uganda. I had wanted to experience something of what it was like to be a night commuter, one of forty thousand boys and girls who, at the height of the war in Northern Uganda, left their homes in remote villages every night to seek refuge in the city's four shelters.

It was eerily quiet as the children flooded onto the road leading into town, and even as an adult, I was uneasy in the growing darkness. The LRA attacked mostly at night, so parents sent their children to the shelters in hopes of protecting them from abduction. After a night's rest, Lily left the Noah's Ark Children's Center every morning at 6:30 and walked to her school, where, like most students her age, she studied chemistry, math, English, and literature. But unlike other teenagers, at the end of her school day, she and her sisters returned home to her village for only an hour or so to wash, eat a small meal, and visit with their parents. Then they walked back to the relative security of the center.

It must have been a relief for Lily's mother that Harriet and Nancy had their older sister to look after them. And she must have taken comfort in the fact that at least the little ones had Lily to tuck them under their blankets at night. But who was there for Lily?

Jesus was. He always is. Even when we are not aware of His presence, He is there, holding our hand. We're not holding His hand; He is holding ours. Otherwise, when we face troubles or temptations, we might let go. We're not strong enough to keep hanging on, and sometimes we don't even want to. But that's just when we most need Him to tighten His grip. And He does.

Take these promises to heart: "As a father has compassion on his children, so the Lord has compassion on those who fear him; for he knows how we are formed, he remembers that we are dust" (Psalm 103:13–14). And though we stumble, we will not fall, for the Lord upholds us with his hand (v. 37:24). In the darkness of the Noah's Ark Children's Center, He holds Lily's hand. In your deepest darkness, He holds yours. And He will never, ever let you go.

—RENEÉ

At sunrise, the children of the Noah's Ark Children's Center dash off to school.

A NEW NEIGHBOR

IF WE ARE IN A POSITION TO HELP SOMEONE IN NEED, WE ARE TO DO EXACTLY THAT.

If anyone has material possessions and sees a brother or sister in need but has no pity on them, how can the love of God be in that person? Dear children, let us not love with words or speech but with actions and in truth.

I JOHN 3:17–18

ON THE EVENING OF DECEMBER 26, 2004, my entire family was nestled in a mountain cabin a few hours from Seattle when I received a news report of a tsunami in South Asia. We had been enjoying our traditional after-Christmas getaway, and I remember thinking how far away South Asia seemed from our snowed-in cabin that night. But that was before I met my distant neighbor Viramuthu. He faced the waves that day in Sri Lanka.

The next morning we drove home, and I spent every waking hour of the following few weeks organizing World Vision's response to the massive human tragedy that followed the waves. A month or so later, I traveled to Sri Lanka and walked along one of the many beaches where the mammoth waves had crested. Hundreds of little flags, fashioned from sticks and scraps of cloth, dotted the beach, marking the places where the dead had

A terrified girl reaches out for her father after a tsunami ravages Sri Lanka in 2004.

been buried right where they had been found. That was the day I met Viramuthu.

Viramuthu and his wife and two daughters had lived on that beach. On that horrifying day, while I was playing board games with my family in a cabin near Seattle, they had been working at their small laundry business. When Viramuthu and his wife saw the thirty-foot wave surging toward them, they each grabbed one of their girls and started to run. As the furious waters engulfed them, Viramuthu saw his wife and daughter disappear even as he and his other daughter made it to safety. Hours later, he found them, arms entwined, hugging each other, lying dead on the beach.

Rubble from a destroyed school covers a beach in Sri Lanka.

I became Viramuthu's neighbor that day; I became his friend. After listening to his tragic story, I put my arm around him and tried to encourage him. And then I looked him in the eye and promised him that World Vision would help him rebuild his life. I would see that his home was rebuilt and his business restored. He knew I could never replace his family, but he smiled through his pain knowing that he would walk this road of recovery with new friends at his side.

We are told in the parable of the good Samaritan that both a priest and a Levite walked along a road and saw a man who had been beaten bloody by robbers and left to die. Even though they saw him, they "passed by on the other side" (Luke 10:31–32). These men who had committed their lives to God were confronted by human suffering then just as we are today. But they walked by the beaten man because he was a stranger. Jesus, however, wants us to see the man not as a stranger but as a neighbor to be loved—loved as much as we love ourselves. The apostle John put it this way: *If anyone has material possessions and sees a brother or sister in need but has no pity on them, how can the love of God be in that person?* Good question.

—Rich

PLEASE PASS
THE SALT

"You are the salt of the earth."

JESUS IN MATTHEW 5:13

I FELT PHYSICALLY ILL listening to the women share with us the horrors they had experienced—stories of abduction, rape, and mayhem at the hands of men who use violence against women as a weapon of war. Over a decade of fear and devastation has ripped apart the very fabric of life for the people of the DRC.

It is estimated that more than one thousand women are raped there every day. One woman told me that the simple act of walking to her field or fetching water makes her a target for warring militias keen on harming those they see as enemy sympathizers. Day after day we heard the stories of ordinary women caught up in the conflict, weeping for lives lost or ruined.

Emotionally drained and overwhelmed by all that I had experienced in the Congo, I met with Robert Kisyula, World Vision Country Director for the DRC, who encouraged me to read 2 Kings 2 and the account of Elisha and the city of Jericho:

A woman weeps as she tells the story of her attack.

The men of the city said to Elisha, "Look, our lord, this town is well situated, as you can see, but the water is bad and the land is unproductive."

"Bring me a new bowl," [Elisha] said, "and put salt in it." So they brought it to him.

Then he went out to the spring and threw the salt into it, saying, "This is what the LORD says: 'I have healed this water. Never again will it cause death or make the land unproductive.'" (vv. 19–21)

Like Jericho, Bob said, the Congo is a land "well situated," brimming with natural resources, and strategically located at a crossroads in the heart of Africa. Could it be that what the Congo needs is a dose of salt? As in Elisha's day, could salt be the answer to the problems our world faces today?

When we think of salt, we think of flavoring. In Elisha's day, salt was also used as a preservative. Either way, the very essence of salt is its ability to transform. It makes flavorless food tasty; it keeps at bay the bacteria that cause decay. In Jericho, salt made bitter water pure and changed unproductive land into fertile ground. Does salt hold the same power today?

It occurs to me that when Jesus told His followers that they were the salt of the earth, He meant that those who claim to know and love the Savior are, like grains of salt, to be transformers of the world into which He's placed them. Some He calls to work for peace and restoration in countries like the Congo. Others He calls to stand up for the truth of the gospel in their homes, their workplaces, and their communities so that all may know the transforming power of the love of Christ.

—Reneé

A survivor of assault in the DRC.

DELIVERING
GOD'S MAIL

**IF WE OPEN OUR EYES, THERE ARE OPPORTUNITIES ALL
AROUND US TO BE AMBASSADORS FOR CHRIST.**

*"The kingdom of heaven is like a king who prepared a
wedding banquet for his son. He sent his servants to those
who had been invited to the banquet to tell them to come, but
they refused to come. Then he sent some more servants and
said, 'Tell those who have been invited that I have prepared
my dinner: My oxen and fattened cattle have been butchered,
and everything is ready. Come to the wedding banquet.'"*

JESUS IN MATTHEW 22:2–4

MOTHER TERESA ONCE SAID, "I am a little pencil in the hand of
a writing God who is sending a love letter to the world." What a great
picture of how God uses us as ambassadors of His great love who deliver
His good news to everyone we encounter.

Jim is a guy in his fifties who delivers the mail at World Vision. Every
day he swings by my office pushing his cart filled with mail. Jim has always
felt pestered by his desire to be a pastor, but life's path took him in different

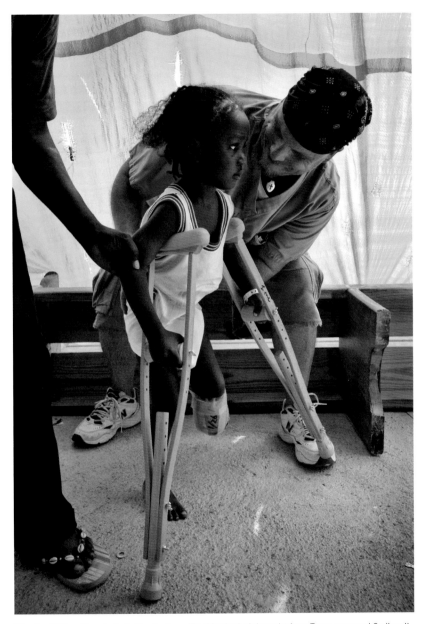

After the 2010 earthquake in Haiti, volunteers like this physical therapist from Texas answered God's call and rushed to help.

directions. He had worked in logistics at SeaTac Airport for twenty-five years and later for a landscaping firm, driving a truck and doing procurement. Desiring to be part of a Christian ministry, he came to work in World Vision's mailroom seven years ago.

When his father-in-law became ill and was moved into a hospice facility to live out his last days, Jim and his wife, Cheryl, often went to visit with him and to pray. During those times Jim began to meet some of the nurses as well as some of the other patients. Perceiving that Jim was a man of faith, nurses began to ask if Jim might get more involved. First they asked if he would lead a regular Sunday worship service for the patients who wished to attend. That blossomed into a ministry of one-on-one meetings as more people started to ask for him for prayer and encouragement.

About a year later, Jim found himself at the center of a thriving ministry. He leads a service every other Sunday for between twenty and forty souls, and, by popular request, he is there quite a few nights and weekends to comfort and pray with people facing the end of their life. One thirteen-year-old girl, after her grandfather passed, followed Jim into the hallway. She grabbed his arm and said, "I need to know. Where did Grandpa go?" Jim was then able to share with her the good news of the gospel.

As Jim's life demonstrates, we don't have to have some big title or influential job or official position to make a difference for Christ. God will use us right where we live if we are willing to be used.

Although a hospice center, with its sights and smells, its ambiance of sickness and death, is not a place most of us want to be. Jim told me this: "I feel like I absolutely have to do this. I would rather be here than anywhere else." He never expected to have such a vital ministry at this stage of his life, but he had made himself available and listened to the Spirit's voice. "I'm just a tool in God's toolbox. I want people to know the good news of Jesus Christ before they die."

You see, Jim knows that the King is inviting people to His great banquet—and Jim wants to be the one to deliver that mail.

—Rich

FOCUS!

"So with you: Now is your time of grief, but I
will see you again and you will rejoice, and no
one will take away your joy."

JESUS IN JOHN 16:22

I CAN REALLY IDENTIFY with the apostle Peter, especially the way he responded when Jesus invited him to step out of the boat and take a walk on the water. Exuberant and full of faith, Peter quickly climbed out and headed toward Jesus. But almost as quickly, Peter turned his attention to the wind and the waves. Instead of keeping his eyes on Jesus, Peter looked at the circumstances around him and, fearing for his life, started to sink. While I've never tried water-walking, I often begin my day joyfully seeking opportunities to serve Jesus, but along the way I get sidetracked, giving in to the temptation to focus on my circumstances rather than on my Savior. But an encounter with a woman who had every reason to be discouraged by her circumstances taught me a powerful lesson I'll never forget.

While visiting an emergency clinic in Maradi, Niger, I stopped to talk with Saa Mamane, a young mother who had come in with her

In a hospital room in the DRC, a mother cares for her son who suffers from malaria.

one-year-old son, Sahabi Ibrahim. Feeding tubes were taped to his nose, and while I watched, a nurse desperately tried to find a vein into which she could insert an IV. The child had been vomiting for days and was so severely dehydrated that when he cried, there were no tears. *Why in the world did she wait so long to bring him to the clinic?* I wondered. With a shrug of resignation, she simply told me that she lived too far away to walk with such a sick baby and that until two days earlier, she hadn't had enough money to come by bus. But when I asked this young woman about her expectations for the future, she immediately brightened. She wanted Sahabi Ibrahim to go to school, to learn English, and to become a nurse so he could return to his village to help others who were sick.

Here was this young mom whose tiny baby was struggling to survive beyond infancy, yet she was making plans for her son's future. Saa Mamane was choosing to focus not on what she lacked—basic necessities like food for her child and adequate medical care for his recovery—but on what she did have: a little boy who, if he survived the famine, just might change the world or at least make a difference for the people of his community.

Saa Mamane faced circumstances so much worse than anything I will ever face, yet she did so with dignity and hope. In contrast, I often allow the little things in life to distract me from focusing on Jesus—even though I know it robs me of my joy. When that happens, I find it helpful to remember that when Peter took his eyes off Jesus and began to sink, Jesus reached out His hand to keep him afloat. When you feel like you're drowning, grab Jesus' hand and refocus!

—RENEÉ

WHY LIVING STARTS
WITH DYING

**ONLY WHEN WE HAVE "DIED TO SELF" DOES NEW LIFE
IN CHRIST SPRING FORTH.**

*We were therefore buried with him through baptism into
death in order that, just as Christ was raised from the dead
through the glory of the Father, we too may live a new life.*

ROMANS 6:4

ONE OF THE HARD TEACHINGS OF SCRIPTURE is the notion that
before we can become alive in Christ, our old self must first die. Most of
us would prefer to hang on to our old self and just add Christ, but that's
not how it works. Jesus asks us to give Him everything in our life that
competes with Him for that number one position.

Perhaps more than any person I have ever known, a woman I met
in the Philippines saw her old life die. Her name is Beng. After losing
everything they had in a typhoon, Beng and her family took refuge in
a cemetery and actually slept among the tombs. To make this macabre
scene even grimmer, the cemetery was bordered by a massive garbage
dump that filled the entire area with the stench of decay. That's where
her children foraged for food each day. Never had I witnessed such

In India, once impoverished women are part of a cooperative that grows and sells oranges to support their children.

appalling conditions. Beng, her family, and the life they had once lived had died.

But after three years of living among the dead, new life began to emerge. Beng had joined a community group and risen to become a leader. She developed a plan to relocate everyone living in the cemetery to a plot of land a few miles away. She successfully petitioned the government for the land, helped fifty families move, and secured the resources to drill a clean water well and bring electricity to this new community. After Beng's old life died, she led her family and community to new life.

I believe Jesus wants each one of us to experience exactly the kind of "death of self" that Beng experienced. Jesus wants you and me to lay our entire life at His feet. So many things compete with God in our life—our career, a family business, or investments we have made. Maybe money, wealth, the ability to create wealth, or the many things money can buy compete with Christ in your life. You might be clinging to an unhealthy relationship, an identity you have carefully shaped, or a reputation you have built. Maybe it's the place you live. Do you love your house, your friends, your comfort, and the familiarity of your life? None of these are bad things unless you place them above God. He wants you to lay all of these things down at His feet and make them available to Him. Now Jesus may not take these things from you, but He does want the certificates of title signed over to Him. He then becomes the Owner and you become the steward, not of your possessions, but of the Master's possessions. Jesus has a new life He wants to give you, but first the old life has to go.

If anyone is in Christ, the new creation has come:
The old has gone, the new is here!

2 CORINTHIANS 5:17

—RICH

THE DOORSTOP

Don't let what you can see weaken your confidence in what you can't.

Elisha prayed, "O Lord, open his eyes so he may see." Then the Lord opened the servant's eyes, and he looked and saw the hills full of horses and chariots of fire all around Elisha.

2 Kings 6:17

YOU KNOW YOU'RE IN TROUBLE WHEN your visit starts out with a briefing by the security officer! At least that's what I thought when I was introduced to Jabs, the man responsible for keeping us safe during our week in the DRC. Having read about the atrocities Congolese women experience, I wanted to see firsthand what was happening in this war-torn country in order to better understand what can be done to help women who find themselves the targets of armed militias. But now I was having second thoughts. Perhaps I had been a bit naive to travel with four other women to a place where rape has become a weapon of war.

And when, at the end of the session, Jabs handed me an old-fashioned wooden doorstop, explaining that it would help prevent someone from forcing his way into my room, it only added to my uncertainty about being there. *Was this simple piece of wood the only thing standing between me*

For Claudine, there was no doorstop. One night rebels came and took her husband away.

and abduction by a militant band of rebels? I hoped not, and yet I had a sinking feeling it was.

We all face uncertainty of one kind or another, not about warring militias perhaps, but about our jobs, our economic futures, our health, our families. It's simply a fact of life that we live in uncertain times, but we don't have to allow that uncertainty to negatively impact our behavior.

Hebrews 11 chronicles people who did not let the uncertainty they faced affect how they lived their lives. Noah built an ark even though, standing in the desert, he saw no evidence of water anywhere. Moses led a band of slaves out of Egypt although it meant giving up the privileges of the house of Pharaoh. One after another the writer to the Hebrews recounts the stories of faithful men and women who, when called upon by God to act, obeyed despite their circumstances.

A child finds refuge at a shelter in the DRC for women who have been raped.

Chapter 11 is called the "Faith Hall of Fame," but the kind of life it describes is not reserved only for the great heroes of our faith. In fact, the people listed would not have considered themselves heroes at all, but ordinary people living out their daily lives "by faith" (Hebrews 11:3). By faith, they did not allow the uncertainty of what they *could* see interfere with their confidence in what they could *not* see. By faith, they relied on what God had already revealed to them about His character; and then believing God's promises, they acted.

When what you see around you threatens to derail your ability to walk by faith, remember what God has already shown you to be true of His character. Then, like those whose names are enshrined in the Faith Hall of Fame, move forward by faith with confidence, knowing that He is at work in ways you may not see.

—Reneé

"TRYING SO HARD"

DO YOUR BEST; THE REST IS UP TO GOD.

Do your best to present yourself to God as one approved,
a workman who does not need to be ashamed and who
correctly handles the word of truth.

2 TIMOTHY 2:15

AS OUR CHILDREN WERE GROWING UP, we—like most parents—tried to communicate to them that we valued *effort* over *outcome*. We wanted to assure them that, regardless of the end result, what was important to us was that they always do their best. It's a simple idea, but as it turns out, it's an idea that's also important to God.

The apostle Paul, in his second letter to Timothy, urged his young friend to do his best. Timothy was encouraged by his father in the faith to work hard to present himself before God as a workman who correctly handled God's Word. Aware of the disputes over doctrine Timothy faced, Paul advised him to act in such a way that he would have no reason to be ashamed.

That advice came to mind as I talked to fourteen-year-old Rith, a young man I met at World Vision's Bamboo Shoots Street Children's Center in Phnom Penh. I asked Rith what he would like teenagers in the

United States to know about him. He said he would like them to know that he is "trying so hard." He is doing his absolute best to be a good student, a responsible brother, a person God can use in the lives of others.

Just a year ago, Rith arrived at the center from the streets of the Cambodian capital, where he had lived with his mother and ten-year-old brother, Roth. Although Rith managed to avoid some of the pitfalls of homelessness like alcohol and drugs, his younger brother has not. Only ten years old, Roth refuses to give up his life on the streets. So, trained by World Vision to be a peer educator, Rith goes out to the street to care for him. On the night I visited, Rith was sitting on a busy corner, across from a casino filled with tourists, surrounded by a group of children. He was showing them pictures illustrating the dangers of living on the streets and sharing with them suggestions for keeping themselves safe. One of the children listening at his feet was Rith's little brother.

Brothers Roth (left) and Rith in Phnom Penh, Cambodia.

Several times a week Rith teaches street children about good hygiene and how to protect themselves against the dangers of living on the streets.

Despite the challenges he faces, Rith is doing his absolute best to use the gifts God has given him to do well in school so he can fulfill his dream of becoming a doctor. He is trying hard to rescue his little brother from a destructive life on the streets. And he is doing all he can to convince the boys and girls he mentors twice a week that there is a better life for them at the center.

Helen Keller is quoted as saying, "When we do the best that we can, we never know what miracle is wrought in our life, or in the life of another." When we apply our best effort to all God has given us to serve Him—to our gifts, talents, time, and opportunities—we, like Rith, can trust the results to Him.

—RENEÉ

WHEN A CHILD DIES

The LORD is near to the brokenhearted
and saves the crushed in spirit.
Many are the afflictions of the righteous,
but the LORD delivers him out of them all.

PSALM 34:18–19 ESV

SADLY, NOT EVERY CHILD helped by World Vision lives "happily ever after." One of the grinding realities we face each day in our work is the appalling rate of child mortality in the developing world.

I know the statistics by heart: one billion people live on less than a dollar a day, another billion drink water contaminated with bacteria and disease, almost a billion are severely malnourished, and—most shocking of all—almost nineteen thousand children die each day of preventable causes. But even knowing these statistics doesn't fully prepare me for coming face-to-face with one of the millions of families who have lost a child.

Tears flowed freely that morning as I sat in the small Guatemala home of Lesbia Arana Valiente and listened to the courageous story of her daughter Marcia. Only twelve years old, Marcia had died of lupus just nine days before. She had been the joy of her mother's life, the eldest of three, and a girl of remarkable strength with a sparkling and optimistic personality.

Through her grief, Lesbia recounted Marcia's long and painful struggle against the disease. It was the story of a mother and father who fought bravely against daunting odds to help their daughter get desperately needed treatments. Imagine the pain of these parents who were turned away by doctors and clinics just because they were poor. Then they turned to World Vision. Even though we got Marcia the best treatment available, she didn't survive.

If we see this story through an earthly lens, World Vision's efforts were in vain; Marcia had become just another statistic. But I reject with all my heart any such conclusion. No act of love and compassion done in the name of Christ is ever in vain. No triumph of the human spirit, even in

After the tsunami in 2004, this heartbroken Indian mother built a shrine to a daughter she will never forget.

death, is a failure. The psalmist wrote that even the righteous will have afflictions but that the Lord is near to the brokenhearted (Psalm 34:18). We trust in a God who is not distant and detached, but intimate and personal; One whom Isaiah described as "a man of sorrows, and familiar with suffering" (v. 53:3). The One who walks with us in our sorrow is the same Jesus who went to the cross for us.

Toward the end of this mother's story of grief, my friend and colleague Scott could no longer contain his emotions. He put his arms around Lesbia and said through his own tears, "You did everything you could. She's with the Lord now. We'll take her story back with us and tell others. We won't forget her."

Even though we live in a world filled with pain and suffering, we are promised the day when every wrong will be righted and every sorrow will turn to joy, when "'He will wipe every tear from their eyes. There will be no more death' or mourning or crying or pain, for the old order of things has passed away" (Revelation 21:4). Jesus won't forget her either.

—RICH

A community in Mozambique buries a sixteen-month-old baby who died of malaria.

I BETTER WRITE
THAT DOWN!

REMEMBERING WHAT GOD HAS DONE IN YOUR PAST WILL HELP YOU TO RELY ON HIS PROMISES FOR THE FUTURE.

We will tell the next generation
the praiseworthy deeds of the LORD,
his power, and the wonders he has done.

PSALM 78:4

WHEN MY CHILDREN WERE LITTLE, it seemed impossible to think I would ever forget a single important event from their childhood. But looking back, I wish I had kept better records. Even pictures don't always jog my memory. Five nearly identical little blonds stare back at me from various photographs as if willing me to recall some significant milestone in their young lives. But often the importance of recording highlights got pushed aside by the daily demands of child rearing. Just imagine how hard it would be to keep a record of your child's growing-up years if you were raising them in a country wracked by war and disease.

But that was exactly what Jane, a young mother of four living in the East African nation of Uganda, was doing. Jane's husband had died of AIDS, and she was working hard as a single mom to raise her children

Jane Nanyungwe, here with daughter Sylvia, keeps a memory book for each one of her four children.

in a difficult environment. In her one room, cinder block home, Jane read to me from a journal she had been keeping of her sons' and daughter's precious childhood memories. As I listened, I was struck by how much Jane's memory book was like the ones I had kept for my children. I was moved by the fact that, despite the challenges of raising a family in Kasamgombe, Uganda, she was still able to enjoy one of the simple pleasures of motherhood: remembering and celebrating the accomplishments of her children.

God places special significance on remembering. Throughout the Old Testament we see the Israelites marking occasions when God demonstrated His faithfulness to them so that future generations would remember what God had done. After Joshua led the people across the Jordan River on dry ground, they gathered twelve stones and built a memorial so that they might not forget what God had done in that place (Joshua 4:20–22). When God brought victory over the Philistine army, "Samuel took a stone and set it up between Mizpah and Shen. He named it Ebenezer, saying, 'Thus far the LORD has helped us'" (1 Samuel 7:12).

Left to their own devices, the Israelites would have forgotten the ways God had faithfully worked in their lives, so they built stone monuments to help them remember that God keeps His promises. Looking back, are there times in your life when God demonstrated His love for you in a very tangible way? Did He bless you with a long-awaited spouse or child, an unexpected recovery from illness, or a new job after a long period of unemployment? Remembering how God has worked in the past can help you move forward with confidence into the future. The Israelites built stone monuments to help them remember. Jane kept a journal. What will you do to remember God's faithfulness in your life so you can move forward with confidence?

—RENEÉ

TREASURE IN HEAVEN

"The kingdom of heaven is like treasure hidden in a field. When a man found it, he hid it again, and then in his joy went and sold all he had and bought that field."

JESUS IN MATTHEW 13:44

HAVE YOU EVER WANTED TO tear a page or two out of your Bible and burn them because you didn't like what they said? That's the way I felt about the story of Jesus and the rich young ruler when I was deliberating over whether I should leave my job as CEO of Lenox china, with all of its perks and prestige, to come to World Vision and serve the poorest of the poor. I'm embarrassed to say that I really wanted to say no to World Vision. God just seemed to be asking too much of me. I could relate to the rich young ruler who had it made: he was wealthy, influential, and confident. He was a faithful Jew and well respected. Perhaps a little puffed up with pride, he asked Jesus whether there was anything he still lacked. Big mistake. This is Jesus' answer: "One thing you lack. . . . Go, sell everything you have and give to the poor, and you will have treasure in heaven.

After selling her most valuable possession to save her mother, Ruse now knows her true value.

Then come, follow me" (Mark 10:21). Really! You can't be serious, Jesus! Everything? Now you see why I wanted to tear that page out of my Bible. Was Jesus really expecting me to *leave everything* and follow Him?

I met a girl in Cambodia, however, who taught me a profound lesson about sacrificial giving. When Ruse was just thirteen, her mother—a single mom of three—became ill and needed money for medical treatment. How would the family afford food, not to mention the doctor's fees? Well, Ruse's neighbor knew a brothel owner who would pay a lot for a young virgin, and that neighbor approached Ruse and her mother with this terrible proposition: sell your virginity and save your mother. As Ruse told us her story, she said something I will never forget: "My virginity was the most valuable possession my family had." So to save her mother, Ruse spent the next three years in a brothel servicing perhaps seven hundred men each year. I find great poignancy in this story of a young girl who

Ruse, whose inexpressible gift of love saved her mother and siblings.

loved so much that she gave herself to save her mother and her siblings. This is the same kind of love that Christ lavished on us: "The Son of Man did not come to be served, but to serve, and to give his life as a ransom for many" (Mark 10:45).

What are the most valuable things you possess? Are you willing to offer them to Jesus? Do you love Him that much? I think that was the issue for the rich young ruler. Jesus didn't really care about the amount of his wealth; Jesus was more concerned with the amount of his love. Jesus wants to fill our life with His treasures, but if our life is filled with other things, we can't receive the gifts from Jesus.

Lenox china filed for bankruptcy just a few years after I left. But since that day when I traded my career for God's calling, my life has overflowed with treasure.

—RICH

LIVING WATER

WHEN WE CHOOSE ANYTHING BUT THE LIVING WATER JESUS OFFERS, WE WILL BE THIRSTY AGAIN.

Leaving her water jar, the woman went back to the town and said to the people, "Come, see a man who told me everything I ever did. Could this be the Christ?"

JOHN 4:28–29

MORNING COMES EARLY when you start your day by walking miles to get water. Not that we didn't have running water in the hotel near the village of Adama, Ethiopia. We did, but we wanted to be at the watering hole when villagers began to gather to fill their buckets from the muddy ditch carved deep into the ground. In this desert community, fetching water is done early in the day, well before the sun has fully risen in the sky. But almost everyone had beaten us to the spot and gone home again. When we arrived, only the children were still there. The smallest of them were actually down in the hole, heads beneath the rim so we couldn't see them until we got right to the edge. They were busy scooping at the little trickle of water bubbling up from underground, putting it in buckets, and then allowing the bigger children to hoist them out.

When the Samaritan woman arrived at the well, it was noon, the hottest part of the day, long past the time when sensible women came to

The watering hole in Boset, Ethiopia.

draw water. But being sensible had nothing to do with her timing. Rather, she waited until the other women had finished filling their buckets before going to the well, perhaps to avoid being reminded of her neighbors' rejection. Imagine her surprise when she found Jesus, a Jewish man, sitting beside the well and, what's more, asking her for a drink of water. It seemed like a simple request, but with those few words Jesus broke down a wall of prejudice and rejection that had separated this woman from the rest of her community for years. And when, confused, she inquired of Him how it was possible that He should ask her for such a thing, He offered her living water.

A ten-year-old boy scoops water from a small pit in Ethiopia.

Her first thought was that she would never have to go to the well again, never have to encounter the stares and rude remarks of others. But instead of keeping this water for herself, the woman put down her water jar and went to summon the rest of her village so that they, too, might have living water. She had gone to the well thirsty; she went away having her thirst fully satisfied by the Messiah, the One who told her everything she had ever done.

Every day the women and children of Adama return to the watering hole in order to satisfy their physical thirst with water that does not last. But there and elsewhere around the world, people are also seeking to quench their spiritual thirst. They return time and again to people, things, and activities that offer only temporary satisfaction. They go from well to well trying to satisfy their longing for love and acceptance by drinking water that will leave them thirsty for more. Only the water that Jesus offers will truly satisfy, so drink deeply from His well.

—Reneé

245

LOVE IN ACTION

GOD CALLS US TO SHARE AN ACTIVE LOVE THAT ENCOURAGES OTHER PEOPLE AND BUILDS THEM UP.

"A new command I give you: Love one another. As I have loved you, so you must love one another. By this everyone will know that you are my disciples, if you love one another."

JESUS IN JOHN 13:34–35

PEOPLE ARE FRAGILE. How often do you watch the news and hear the story of a person whose life was changed in an instant: an automobile accident, a financial reversal, a divorce, a cancer diagnosis, or maybe a wildfire, tornado, or flood that took away their home in just minutes. The human spirit is so very fragile.

In 2000, Mozambique was inundated with devastating floods that left tens of thousands homeless and vulnerable. I traveled there to see what help they needed, and Rosa became, for me, the very face of human vulnerability. Rosa, her four children, and her husband watched in horror as the waters rose from their knees, to their waists, to their necks. Pushing each of her children into a tree, Rosa climbed up behind them to safety. Her husband was washed downstream and managed to climb into a second tree. From those trees, they watched all that they owned be destroyed: first their crops, just a week from harvest; and then their

World Vision staff, like Jean Marie Mugwaneza, put love into action after the Rwandan genocide.

livestock—goats, chickens, cows, and ducks; and finally their house. For a poor family like Rosa's, this was their only wealth, their security, accumulated painstakingly over years. Rosa spent four nights and five days in that tree. That she even had the will to cling to life with her children after such a loss is remarkable. The human spirit is also very strong.

The entire family now lived under a plastic tarp in a transit center. They had lost more than their home and their livelihood; they had also lost their dignity and their hope. And they would need some help to rebuild their life; they couldn't do it by themselves. Jesus understood loss. That's why He touched the leper, welcomed the prostitute, showed mercy to the woman caught in adultery, and healed the crippled and the blind. He touched, healed, loved, cared, and even wept when confronted with human brokenness and vulnerability. And then He went to the cross so all who are broken might again be whole. Jesus restores, reclaims, and redeems. We could not do it by ourselves. And after Jesus rebuilds us, then He sends us, healed and restored, to take hope and healing to others, to be His hands and feet. Love in action, not just words, because people are fragile. We can't do it by ourselves.

Rosa and her family would need a rebuilt home, livestock, and seeds to plant. They would need more than a handout; they would need a hand up. They would need their hope restored. Who do you see that is broken? Who has lost their job or their home? Who has lost hope? Has sickness stricken a neighbor? Has someone's child made a bad choice? Wipe a tear. Give a hug. Hold a hand. Be their hope. Be their healing. Be the one who encourages and restores. Be Jesus with skin on. "Let us not love with words or speech but with actions and in truth" (1 John 3:18).

—RICH

Three sisters made homeless by the Haiti earthquake in 2010.

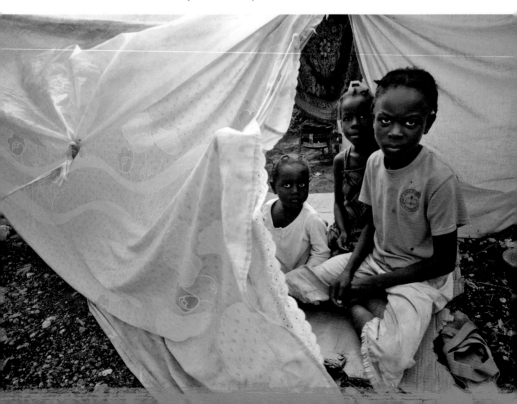

GREAT EXPECTATIONS

TAKE YOUR DEEPEST DESIRES TO GOD.

Give ear to my words, O LORD,
consider my sighing.
Listen to my cry for help,
my King and my God,
for to you I pray.
In the morning, O LORD, you hear my voice;
in the morning I lay my requests before you
and wait in expectation.

PSALM 5:1–3

IT WAS A RARE autumn day in Seattle, crisp, cool, not a raincloud in sight. Like so many other moms at that time of year, I was sitting in the bleachers watching one of my children play soccer. When my cell phone rang, I was greeted by the panicked voice of my oldest daughter, Sarah.

"Mom, can you come home? I fell down the stairs, and there's blood everywhere!"

In less than an hour, we'd seen the family physician who closed the gash in Sarah's shin with a neat row of twenty stitches and were headed home with antibiotics to prevent infection. Everything we needed had been available to us, almost immediately. Not so for Haoua Seine, a mother I'd met

Men and women seek a rare spot of shade in the midst of a drought in Zimbabwe, waiting for lifesaving food at a distribution center.

just four days earlier in the West African country of Niger. She'd brought her small son to greet me as I was visiting a World Vision Area Development Project on the outskirts of Niamey, the capital city. The boy appeared to have a poultice stuck to his foot, made of something that looked suspiciously like mashed potatoes.

"What happened to this little boy?" I asked through the translator.

"He fell in the fire."

"Has he seen a doctor?"

"No, his mother is using traditional medicines."

No cell phone plea for help, no frantic drive to a doctor's office, just a mixture of herbs and an expectation that her son's wound would eventually heal.

Down the road in the village of Doukoukouneye, I stood with women lined up to receive their monthly rations from a World Food Programme distribution. A flash flood had wiped out the only road into the village, and the truck containing supplies was delayed. As a result, most had waited more than seven hours in temperatures that exceeded 100°F to receive their rations—a mosquito net, four bars of soap, and a bag of millet. But no one complained. They had faith that, sooner or later, the food would arrive. And arrive it did, to songs of joy and exuberant dancing. They were grateful for what they received, not annoyed that it had taken so long.

Theirs was not a spirit of entitlement, of unreasonable demands. Rather Haoua Seine and the women of Doukoukouneye displayed a quiet confidence that God would come to their aid. Is that your response when you encounter difficult circumstances, or do you, like me, sometimes give in to the temptation to complain? How much better to put aside our own attitudes of entitlement and follow the example of King David who, when facing an enemy bent on destroying him, boldly took his needs to his Father in prayer, unshakable in his expectation that God would act. The apostle Paul spoke of prayer as "earnest labor" (Colossians 4:12 NASB). When you are tempted to complain, roll up your sleeves and likewise, with great expectation, take your deepest desires to God, confident in His character and His power to meet all your needs.

—RENEÉ

PROVOKING THE QUESTION

OUR MOST POWERFUL WITNESS IS OFTEN THE TESTIMONY OF OUR LIVES AND WORDS.

"In the same way, let your light shine before others, that they may see your good deeds and glorify your Father in heaven."

JESUS IN MATTHEW 5:16

I REMEMBER IT BEING UNBEARABLY HOT THAT DAY . . .

It was about six months after the devastating Gujarat earthquake that took twenty thousand lives in India and destroyed some three million homes. I was participating in a ceremony to celebrate the joint effort of World Vision and Habitat for Humanity to rebuild hundreds of houses. The entire community was gathered to express their thanks for the help they had received.

During the ceremony, a group of turbaned village elders, with deeply lined faces and magnificent white beards, sat just a few yards behind us observing and discussing everything that was happening. One of my colleagues, who spoke Hindi happened to overhear their conversation. They were asking themselves why these Christians had come from ten thousand miles away to help them when they had not received much help

A volunteer from the US helps build a home in Honduras.

from their own government or religious leaders. They were wondering what had motivated complete strangers to help them. It would be clear to them in the minutes that followed that we had been motivated by the love of Christ.

When we think of Jesus' command to take the gospel to all nations, we tend to think in terms of large efforts: evangelistic crusades, *The Jesus Film*, and global radio broadcasts. But the most powerful witness for the gospel is often the testimony of our life, how we live out our faith each day in front of other people. At World Vision we sometimes call this "provoking the question": it's living and acting in such a way that people have to ask why we seem so different. If you look at the life of Jesus, the chief reason people listened to Him at all was because of His actions: He healed the sick, spent time with the outcasts, and lifted the spirits of the downtrodden. No one had ever lived as Jesus did. No one had ever been so compassionate, so caring, so inclusive. His life and his words spoke of a different way to live.

A couple of years back my son Pete had parked for just a few minutes in a "No Parking" zone. When he came out, his car had been towed, and Pete learned a very expensive lesson. When he went to

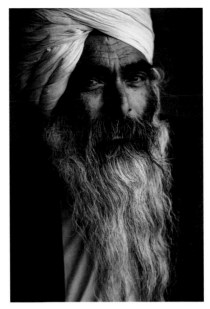

How we live our lives provokes the question: Why?

the impound lot to pay, he was angry and gave the attendant a piece of his mind. But a few hours later he became convicted about his behavior. So Pete drove all the way back to apologize to the man for his angry words. He explained that he is a Christian and that his behavior had been inappropriate. (This was probably the first apology the man had ever received from a customer!) While it might have been better not to have vented his anger in the first place, I am sure Pete's apology provoked the question, "Why is this kid so different?"

What will you do in your life so that every day, you "provoke the question?"

Someone once said, "Endeavor to live so that when you die even the undertaker will be sorry." Good advice.

—RICH

LONE RANGER CHRISTIANS

SEEK OUT THE FELLOWSHIP OF OTHER BELIEVERS.

Let us not give up meeting together, as some are in the habit of doing, but let us encourage one another—and all the more as you see the Day approaching.

HEBREWS 10:25

FOR ALL OF THE THIRTY-EIGHT YEARS Rich and I have been married, we've been members of a couples' small-group Bible study. We've lived in three states and various cities, but we've never gone very long without joining a group of believers committed to studying God's Word together. We know how much we need to be part of a body that supports, encourages, and prays for one another, and we take seriously the admonition by the writer to the Hebrews to spend time with others who share our faith.

But a group of women I met in Senzani, Malawi, take obedience to this instruction to a whole new level. Talk about encouragers! When I met them, they were gathered around a giant pot of pumpkin leaves they were preparing for their friend Rabecca, a young mother of two who was dying of AIDS. She'd been abandoned by the husband who'd infected her with the disease,

Reneé reads to Rabecca's daughter, Shailey.

and she was struggling to keep her household afloat. Enter these three women from the local church, who daily prepared her meals, bathed her frail body, and cared for her two children, ages ten and three. Since Rabecca was isolated from others because of her disease, they were her only community, offering a mixture of practical service and spiritual and emotional support not unlike that of first-century believers.

Faced with pressure and persecution from the outside world, early Christians banded together to encourage, strengthen, and help one another grow in faith. In Acts 2 we see a church where believers "devoted themselves to the apostles' teaching and to fellowship, to the breaking of bread and to prayer" (v. 42).

So why, in this context, did the writer to the Hebrews feel it necessary to warn the early church not to abandon meeting together? What would cause them to forsake Christian community? For some, it was

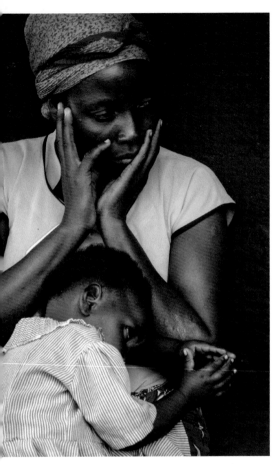

Rabecca, with daughter Tamandani, would be lost without community support.

likely the growing risk of persecution. But others may have simply succumbed to the temptation to go it alone, to become self-sufficient. To them, the writer to the Hebrews says, "Don't do it! You need other people!" As believers, we are all part of the body of Christ, and the body can't work the way God designed it unless all the parts work together. As Paul said to the church at Corinth, "The eye cannot say to the hand, 'I don't need you!' And the head cannot say to the feet, 'I don't need you!'" (1 Corinthians 12:21). We need each other in the very same way that Rabecca needed the pumpkin leaf ladies!

So resist the temptation to become a Lone Ranger Christian. Don't isolate yourself from others. Follow the example of those early believers who knew the importance of living in community. Seek out the fellowship of those who will encourage you in your desire to grow and become more like the Savior. Remember, even the Lone Ranger needed the encouragement of his trusty companion, Tonto!

—RENEÉ

DYING TO SELF

**WE ONLY TRULY DIE TO SELF AS WE BECOME
MORE AND MORE LIKE CHRIST.**

*Blessed is the one who perseveres under trial because,
having stood the test, that person will receive the crown
of life that the Lord has promised to those who love him.*

JAMES 1:12

C. S. LEWIS ONCE SAID, "Humility is not thinking less of yourself but thinking of yourself less." We have come to think of humility in terms of modesty about our accomplishments rather than as a way of living that puts the needs of others ahead of our own. But biblical humility—the kind Christ demonstrated—calls us to empty ourselves of self-interest and to fill ourselves with the Spirit of Christ who "made himself nothing by taking the very nature of a servant" (Philippians 2:7). For most of us this dying to self doesn't come naturally; in fact, we must choose to die to self. And progress is a lifelong journey.

A few years ago Reneé and I met a woman in India who lived out just this kind of Christlikeness. Mary* had every reason to throw herself a pity party. She had been infected with HIV by an unfaithful husband who then deserted her and her three children. She soon succumbed to full-blown AIDS and dwindled to little more than a walking skeleton.

---

* Name changed to protect identity.

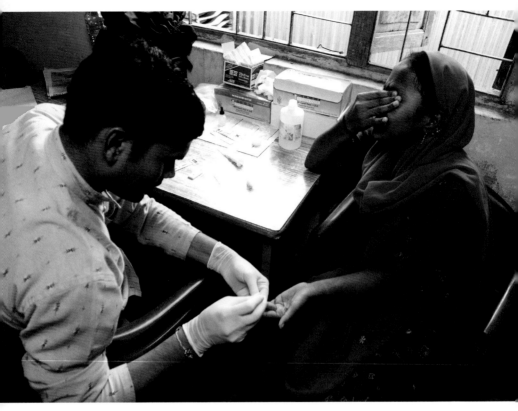

THIS PAGE AND FACING PAGE: Testing for HIV in India.

When we met her she was shockingly close to death and confined to her sweltingly hot fifth-floor flat located just across from a slaughterhouse that filled the apartment with the awful smell of death. In this squalid place, Mary was bedridden but surrounded by those who loved her: her elderly mother and her three young children. During our visit, Mary's kids—probably sensing what was happening—couldn't stop hugging their mom.

There was no sense of a "Why me?" attitude in Mary. She showed no anger or bitterness or evidence that she felt her circumstances were unfair or undeserved. She mostly exhibited a concern for others. "I don't ask you to pray for me," she told us, "but I want you to pray for my children and my mother. And I want you to help the other women and orphans out there who are suffering and have no one to help them."

We live in a culture that preaches an appealing gospel of entitlement and personal rights, and that way of thinking can easily seep into our faith, compelling us to seek a God of blessing who answers our prayers for happiness and comfort. But Mary lived in a world of poverty and exclusion; she had no expectation of privilege or freedom from want. Yet she prayed to a God who also knows suffering, to the One who "was despised and rejected by mankind, a man of suffering, and familiar with pain" (Isaiah 53:3). She found comfort in the One who "was pierced for our transgressions," "crushed for our iniquities," and by whose "wounds we are healed" (v. 5). Mary met her Savior in the midst of her suffering; it was there she found her Lord and Friend.

Might it be that we seek Him in all the wrong places?

—RICH

A MOM LIKE ME

THE GOOD NEWS OF GOD'S KINGDOM IS FOR EVERYONE!

Jesus called the children to him and said, "Let the little children come to me, and do not hinder them, for the kingdom of God belongs to such as these."

LUKE 18:16

WE STOOD TOGETHER AT THE EDGE of El Basurero, the Guatemala City dump, my clothes getting dirty from the debris churned up by the coming and going of the garbage trucks. Juana was dressed not so much in clothing as in pieces of cloth secured about her with rope, a nursing baby at her breast. It was 1998, and I was on my very first trip to see World Vision's work in the field. We were on our way to visit a day care center for the children of families who scavenged the dump for bits of recyclable plastic or a leftover bite of sandwich. But first we stopped to see the place so many of Guatemala's poor called home. Juana's son was eating contentedly from a dirt-encrusted yogurt container he'd found among the debris, and as I bent to admire her beautiful little boy, I could see in her smile the pride she had in her family, the pleasure she took in seeing her children the focus of my attention. As a mother, I know those feelings.

The Guatemala City dump makes for a hard day of labor for a child.

Across the street at the day care center, I met forty children who would spend the day not at the dump, but in a place where boys and girls received a hot meal, sang songs, and learned about Jesus. I wondered why Juana's children were not among this happy group. I could only imagine that she may have been reluctant to allow her children to attend, perhaps fearful of letting out of her sight the only thing she could truly call her own.

I was new to such a situation and uncomfortable, overwhelmed by the stench of the dump, the filth, the desperately poor. So I stood there, silent. But looking back, I wish I had shared with Juana the hope she would find inside the walls of that nursery school. I could have told her that through the doors of the day care center were people who saw caring for children as an act of worship and service to God, people who shared the message that beyond the poverty, beyond the dump, there is good news.

What good news could they possibly have for Juana, a woman whose life was defined by the hard realities of El Basurero? It is the same good news that is available to you and to me. It's the good news that, no matter

Fighting vultures for valuables at the Guatemala City dump.

how bleak the circumstances we find ourselves in, God loves us so much that He sent His one and only Son to die on a cross so that we can experience new life through faith in Him. I know she would have responded. She's a mom ... like me.

—RENEÉ

GOING AGAINST
YOUR INSTINCTS

RESPONDING WITH KINDNESS TO THOSE WHO HURT US WILL OFTEN CHANGE THE WHOLE EQUATION.

"If your enemy is hungry, feed him;
if he is thirsty, give him something to drink.
In doing this, you will heap burning coals on his head."
Do not be overcome by evil, but overcome evil with good.

ROMANS 12:20–21

REGASSA HATED CHRISTIANS, and he hated World Vision. When World Vision applied to the local government for a piece of land for an irrigation project in Regassa's community in Ethiopia, he found himself responsible for assigning the land. So he gave the worst possible piece of land: a graveyard. He even launched a smear campaign, going from farmer to farmer to speak against the project.

But then Regassa's life fell apart. For six years he was bedridden with a series of illnesses, and he ended up losing all of his assets. Then his wife died unexpectedly, leaving him as a widower with several children. He was so poor he didn't even have the water he needed to wash his wife's body to prepare her for burial. But World Vision heard about his

Regassa's hatred for Christians ran so deep, he even hated World Vision's vehicles. Today he is the transformed father of six-year-old Abraham.

suffering and offered Regassa a helping hand. His hatred was answered with love.

Over time Regassa received tools to plant new crops and other help he needed to get back on his feet. His heart began to soften. He then attended a spiritual conference hosted by World Vision. There he found new friends and new hope, his illnesses went away, and he committed his life to Christ. Today Regassa is remarried and has two more children. His farming has prospered, he was named "Best Model Farmer" by his community, and he was selected to serve as an elder in his church. Hatred had been answered with kindness.

Maybe we can't relate directly to the kind of hatred Regassa felt, but we can all relate to being hurt by someone or treated unfairly. I was once passed over for a promotion I had earned. But the VP of marketing announced that a guy named Phil—from a different department altogether and with no relevant experience—would get the job. The situation felt unfair, and it hurt. I had paid my dues, and I deserved that job. I couldn't change the decision, but I could decide how I'd respond. A week or so later I ran into the VP who had treated me so unfairly. He nervously said, "How's it going, Rich?" I looked him in the eye and said, "It's going great! Phil is a great guy, and I'm teaching him the things he needs to know. We are going to be a solid team." No doubt expecting an angry tirade from me, he seemed quite startled—and relieved. Six months

Regassa's son, Abraham.

later he called me into his office. Another big job had opened up, and he offered it to me. He told me, "That day in the hallway six months back— that's when I realized the kind of leader you could be. You deserve this!"

When someone does something hurtful to us or treats us unfairly, our first instinct is to strike back, to get even, to hurt them as well. But that is not the way of Jesus. So compliment the one who criticizes you. Forgive the one who judges you. Help the one who hurts you. *Overcome evil with good.*

—RICH

AN ACCEPTABLE
SACRIFICE

**THE GIFTS WE GIVE TO OTHERS CAN BE AN EXPRESSION
OF OUR GRATITUDE TO GOD.**

*I have received full payment and even more; I am amply
supplied, now that I have received from Epaphroditus the
gifts you sent. They are a fragrant offering, an acceptable
sacrifice, pleasing to God.*

PHILIPPIANS 4:18

WE WERE RUNNING VERY LATE. This was to be the last stop of the
day, but with each previous stop we'd made along the way, we had fallen
progressively behind. We were so late, in fact, I half expected the mothers'
group we were meeting to be gone. But when we rounded the corner of the
school yard a few miles outside of Lima, Peru, I was amazed to see several
hundred women lined up to greet us with gifts of flowers, food, and notes
of thanks. One of them, a young mother named Maria, had even brought
a needlework sampler she'd made for me, representing hours of labor for
someone she didn't even know.

What could have prompted this generosity? Why were these women so
intent on sharing with complete strangers what little they had? Of course

they appreciated the impact microfinance loans had made on their families, and they valued the computer training their children were receiving. But more than that, these tangible expressions of gratitude were "a fragrant offering, an acceptable sacrifice, pleasing to God" (Philippians 4:18).

That's what the apostle Paul called the gifts he received from the church at Philippi. Poor and persecuted, the Philippians nonetheless sought to provide for Paul's needs, and Paul was filled with gratitude. Their gifts were evidence of their partnership in the work of the gospel and confirmation of the "good work" that God was doing in their lives (v. 1:6). By giving to him, Paul said, it was as if the Philippians were giving to God.

Similarly, when I received the needlework sampler from Maria, I knew it wasn't for me. It wasn't even for the World Vision staff and donors we represented. Rather, out of the overflow of her heart, Maria gave this elaborate gift in gratitude to Jesus. Like Mary, who anointed Jesus' feet

A microenterprise loan yielded a multitude of gifts for this women's group in Guatemala—the opportunity to earn an income and the chance to share laughter.

A women's health cooperative jumps for joy in Bolivia.

with perfume (John 12:3), Maria's gift was an extravagant sacrifice given with thanksgiving to God for what He had done in her life and in the life of her family.

God doesn't need our gifts, but like Maria, Mary, and the Philippian church, it's good for us to give them as an expression of our gratitude to Him who has given us all things. We need to give—not just our money, but also our time, our influence, our prayers, our praise. When we confess the name of Jesus to a hurting world and share with those in need around us, we give back to God a fragrant offering, an acceptable sacrifice. So "let us continually offer to God a sacrifice of praise—the fruit of lips that confess His name. And do not forget to do good and to share with others, for with such sacrifices God is pleased" (Hebrews 13:15–16).

—Reneé

ARE YOU
CONTAGIOUS?

WE HAVE THE ABILITY TO TOUCH THE LIVES OF MANY PEOPLE, AND OUR TOUCH IS POWERFUL. BUT WHAT DOES OUR TOUCH COMMUNICATE?

A man with leprosy came to [Jesus] and begged him on his knees, "If you are willing, you can make me clean." Filled with compassion, Jesus reached out his hand and touched the man. "I am willing," he said. "Be clean!" Immediately the leprosy left him and he was cured.

MARK 1:40–42

MAHESHWARI SEEMED TO BE A HEALTHY forty-two-year-old with a contagious smile when I met her a few years back in Chennai, India. But her body carried a contagious disease. Maheshwari learned she had HIV when her husband died of AIDS. As she spiraled downward into full-blown AIDS, she became emaciated, and she had to beg her parents to take her back in. They did, but fearing her disease, they made her live and sleep outside their small house on a cement porch. Once, when Maheshwari fell going to the toilet and cried for help, her own mother—filled with fear and revulsion—would not touch her. Instead she offered Maheshwari a stick to grab so she could pull her daughter back up.

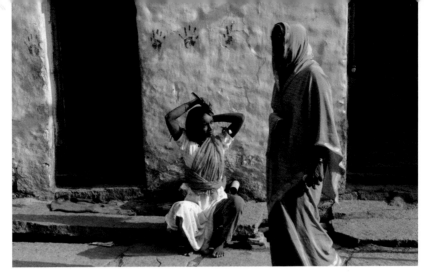

Like Maheshwari, Sudha's mother was infected with HIV in India. When their mother died, Sudha and her brother received help from World Vision.

When the unclean leper approached Jesus, He did the unthinkable to the one who was untouchable: "Filled with compassion, [Jesus] reached out his hand and touched the man." Jesus was not filled with judgment or fear, not with loathing and disgust, not with coldness or indifference—but with *compassion*. It was not the leper's disease that was contagious that day; it was the compassion of Jesus.

One day Christopher, a World Vision program manager, received a phone call: a woman at Maheshwari's address was dying. He went to the house and found Maheshwari moaning and lying behind a door. "I couldn't believe it," he said. "She was just a bundle of cloth and rags." When he bent down and reached out his hand to touch her, she broke down crying. "It was the first time that someone had touched me, knowing I'm with AIDS," she told me. Christopher's compassion was contagious too that day.

What about you? You touch the lives of hundreds of people in the course of your daily life, and they each touch hundreds of others. Are you contagious? If so, just what virus are you spreading? Does your touch spread only judgment or cynicism, superiority or disdain, pessimism or indifference? Or is yours the healing touch of the love of Christ, spreading compassion, joy, affirmation, inclusion, encouragement, optimism, and comfort? Our touch always spreads something.

Maheshwari found help and healing in Christopher's touch. She got treatment, and she got well. As she lay recovering, blessed by the tender care of Christian workers, she loved to listen to them singing and praying. "Just watching and listening to these women made me want to live again," Maheshwari told me.

Having felt the touch of Jesus through the compassion of His servants, Maheshwari is paying it forward. Today she works as a counselor, encouraging women who are suffering as she once did. *Filled with compassion, she now uses her hands to touch others with the same loving touch of Jesus.* Maheshwari is contagious again. In fact, she wants to start an epidemic: "I just want to pass on the message of caring for other people."

—RICH

In India, while shame is still strongly associated with AIDS, a healing touch can bring comfort and spread compassion.

HUMAN PACK ANIMALS

"Are you tired? Worn out? Burned out on religion? Come to me. Get away with me and you'll recover your life. I'll show you how to take a real rest. Walk with me and work with me—watch how I do it. Learn the unforced rhythms of grace. I won't lay anything heavy or ill-fitting on you. Keep company with me and you'll learn to live freely and lightly."

JESUS IN MATTHEW 11:28–30 MSG

VOLCANIC ROCK STILL COVERS the roads of Goma, a reminder of the 2002 eruption of Mount Nyirangongo. The stream of volcanic material that flowed into the capital of this eastern province of the DRC was up to six feet deep in parts of the city. What remains is a landscape difficult to traverse except on foot. As a result, transportation is limited, and the movement of goods through the city is often left to women acting as human pack mules.

They work as porters, carrying up to two hundred pounds of cassava flour, charcoal, or wood on their backs, the giant loads secured with ropes

Sometimes bearing loads up to two hundred pounds, women porters in the DRC make their way to market.

tied around their foreheads. Most earn less than two dollars a day; many of them, less than a dollar.

We gathered at the home of Mama Jeanette to meet several of these women. One had been the wife of a school principal, but after his death, she began working as a porter to support her family, standing all day outside the market waiting for customers. Mama Jeanette told us she often sought her out because Mama Jeanette's groceries were lighter than the other loads this frail woman might be hired to carry. I can only imagine that when she saw Mama Jeanette in the crowd, her face would brighten because she knew that at least for a little while, the weight she bore would be more manageable, a little less burdensome.

Jesus also seeks out people who are exhausted from their heavy burdens—disappointment, loneliness, anxiety, guilt. He invites us to exchange these overwhelming loads for something easier to carry; He

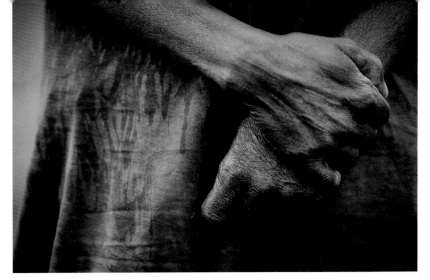

The hands of a Congolese woman laborer reflect her hard life.

calls us to lay down our own heavy yokes and to take up His. The people of Israel knew the yoke of slavery from their days in Egypt; they knew the yoke of legalism the Pharisees attempted to impose. But Jesus' yoke is different. The yoke Jesus invites us to take is that of discipleship. Through the Holy Spirit dwelling in every Christ-follower, His yoke equips us to walk with Him, to live in this world as Jesus would.

When I think back to the porters assembled in Mama Jeanette's home, I'm reminded of Jesus as He went throughout the villages teaching and healing the sick. "When he saw the crowds, he had compassion on them, because they were harassed and helpless, like sheep without a shepherd" (Matthew 9:36). Gentle, humble, compassionate Jesus longs to lead His flock into green pastures where we might be released from whatever it is that weighs us down. Then, refreshed and equipped, He sends us back into the world as His ambassadors.

In the Greek Orthodox tradition, *Theotokos* or "God-bearer" was a title given to Mary, the mother of Jesus. We, too, are God-bearers: the load we are to bear is the good news of Jesus Christ in a world that so desperately needs to know His healing love and saving grace.

—RENEÉ

WORKING FOR CHRIST

CONSIDER WORK A BLESSING: GOD MADE YOU IN HIS OWN IMAGE AND WANTS YOU TO USE YOUR GIFTEDNESS AS AN OFFERING TO HIM.

Whatever you do, work at it with all your heart, as working for the Lord, not for human masters, since you know that you will receive an inheritance from the Lord as a reward. It is the Lord Christ you are serving.

COLOSSIANS 3:23–24

ACCORDING TO RECENT SURVEYS less than 50 percent of Americans are happy in their jobs.

Back in the days when I was working in the corporate world, I often complained about my job, my boss, my pay, the long hours—until one day I had no job at all. Over a period of about two years, I lost my job twice; I spent fourteen months out of work, wishing I had a job to complain about! Perspective was everything.

Lida Sargsyan also longed for a job. After the fall of communism, Lida and most of the people in her country struggled to make ends meet in Armenia's collapsing economy. Those were hard times, for nothing robs a person of his or her dignity more than not being able to support oneself

Mt. Ararat looms behind Khor Virap monastery—foundational to Armenian Christianity.

or one's family. Lida was very creative and had lots of ideas but no way to make them flower . . . until one day she applied for a microloan. With that money, she bought a sewing machine and some fabric and started to sew. Over the next few years she sewed and sewed—and watched her ideas come to life. When I met Lida, her clothing business employed forty people, and her factory filled an entire building. The warehouse was filled with orders waiting to ship not only locally but internationally as well. Her dignity now restored, Lida beamed with pride over what she had accomplished by using the gifts God had given her.

I believe that God wants each of us to take exactly that kind of pride in our work, no matter what that work is. The Almighty created us in His image, filling us with gifts, talents, ideas, and creativity. But if we are working only to serve ourselves, if we are working solely for our own advancement, we will never be fully satisfied.

So consider work from this perspective: followers of Christ should make no distinction between the sacred and the secular. All work is sacred if it does not violate God's laws and if it is offered in the service of building His kingdom. God's "calling" on our life is a calling away from our own agendas, often a leaving behind of our hopes and dreams to embrace His hopes and dreams for our lives. It is a putting to death of our purposes and priorities at the same time that it is a coming alive to God's purposes and priorities. So we should see our work, whatever it might be, as a vehicle for serving God: "It is the Lord Christ [we] are serving."

When I finally found a job after my long unemployment, I began each day with this prayer: "Lord, how can I love, serve, and obey You here, today, in this place?" That simple prayer helped me approach my day as one great opportunity to be an ambassador for Christ. And I could be His ambassador as a cabdriver or a CEO. The job didn't matter as long as I was doing the work for Him. Perspective, again, was everything.

—RICH

TIME FOR DINNER!

FEAR CAN KEEP US FROM EXPERIENCING ALL THAT GOD HAS IN STORE FOR US.

For I am the LORD, your God,
who takes hold of your right hand
and says to you, Do not fear. . . .

ISAIAH 41:13

I LOVE TO COOK, and I enjoy trying out new recipes, so when I travel, I visit local grocery stores to see what kinds of foods are available. And when I enter the homes of families kind enough to invite me into their lives for a few hours, we almost always share a meal. Eating is just one of those activities that brings people together. It's a relationship builder. Sitting around a table for a meal breaks down barriers, especially when the food, or the manner in which it's eaten, is unique to the place where it's served.

I'll never forget the long gray eel undulating across a platter in Northern China. Or the communal dish in Ethiopia, eaten only with our hands, full of the fieriest food I've ever put in my mouth. Most unusual was the fermented beverage we drank from a bowl passed from person to person around the table as we sat inside a tent in the middle of Mongolia. Only later did I learn it was horse's milk.

In kitchens around the world, such as this one in Zimbabwe, breaking bread together inspires trust.

Significant things happened when people in the Bible sat down to break bread together. Think of the meal served to the angelic visitors who came to announce that Sarah and Abraham would have a son (Genesis 18), the miraculous provision of flour and oil for the widow of Zarephath (1 Kings 17), the feeding of the five thousand (Matthew 14), and the recommissioning of Peter at a barbecue on the beach (John 21).

Cambodian fish delicacy.

Meals still offer important opportunities for forging bonds, building friendship, encouraging others. So imagine my discomfort when, while sitting in a local pastor's home in rural Guatemala, the women with whom I traveled refused to eat the food his wife had prepared for us. In their defense, it was their first trip outside the United States, and they were reluctant to join in the meal, afraid they might become ill. I compensated for their lack of enthusiasm by eating more than my fair share.

My friend used to travel to Vietnam several times a year. Her mantra was "Where He leads, I will follow. What He feeds, I will swallow." I think those are pretty good words to live by. Absent from her wise counsel is the fear that kept my traveling companions in Guatemala from enjoying a meal with the pastor's wife. Rather, her advice is characterized by confidence—not in herself, but in the One who sent her.

Fear holds us back. It keeps us from stepping out of our comfort zones and into the great adventure of life. Granted, fear might help us avoid a plate of eel or a bowl of horse's milk, but it also might just cause us to miss something incredible that God has in store for us. So fear not!

—RENEÉ

SEVEN STEPS TO POVERTY

LOVING OUR NEIGHBORS AS OURSELVES FIRST REQUIRES US TO WALK A FEW STEPS IN THEIR SHOES.

"Do not seek revenge or bear a grudge against one of your people, but love your neighbor as yourself. I am the LORD."

LEVITICUS 19:18

IN THIS BOOK RENEÉ AND I HAVE INTRODUCED YOU to some of God's beloved poor, but without meeting them in person, it's hard to fully grasp what their poverty actually feels like. So I'd like to take you on a mental and emotional journey into poverty. Follow me as, one at a time, I take seven things away from you. And let yourself feel the pain of the poor.

First, I will take away your **clothes**. Don't panic, I won't take them all. You can keep the ones you're wearing. Can you imagine wearing the same clothes every single day? You can wash them each night, but even this small takeaway is humiliating.

Next, I will take away **electricity** and **power**. Imagine going home to a dark house each night. None of your appliances work: you can't use your refrigerator, telephone, heater, air conditioner, dishwasher, television, computer, or stove. Your showers are cold, and now you have to wash your clothes by hand. *Inconvenient* is an understatement. But you shouldn't feel too bad; you are still better off than most of the world.

Takeaway number three is really tough: I'm taking away your **clean water**. Now none of your faucets, toilets, or showers work, and your only water source is a stagnant water hole about a mile away. You must walk hours each day to fetch the water your family needs, and because it is teeming with bacteria, you and your children are constantly sick. Making this situation even harder is the fact that none of your neighbors have been affected, and they don't even seem to notice your suffering.

A Burundian girl looks outside from her mud and leaf hut, perhaps hoping for a better future.

I'm afraid I now have to take away your **home**, so you have to live in a ten-by-twenty-foot mud hut with a dirt floor, no beds, and little furniture. Your whole family will now sleep in the same room on the floor.

Takeaway number five is devastating: **food**. Long ago your children lost their smiles; now they are so hungry that the gnawing pain won't go away. You have to find what little food you can by picking through your neighbors' garbage. Already sick from drinking dirty water, your children become malnourished, and their bodies can't fight off diseases. Your four-year-old daughter seems to be slipping away.

Getting her to the doctor is urgent but, tragically, the sixth takeaway is **health care**. To your horror and disbelief, there is no doctor and you have no option except to watch powerlessly as your daughter, wracked with parasites and diarrhea, dies before your very eyes! How can this be happening?

A boy's shirt bears witness to Burundi's long civil conflict.

So what else could I possibly take away? Takeaway number seven is **hope**. Your hope has died in the ashes of your poverty. And you wonder why no one has stepped in to help you.

Do these seven takeaways make you feel compelled to do something about the hardships that billions of people endure each day?

> *If anyone has material possessions and sees a brother*
> *or sister in need but has no pity on them, how can the*
> *love of God be in him?*

I JOHN 3:17

—RICH

STARRY, STARRY NIGHT

DON'T LET BUSYNESS CROWD OUT GOD'S VOICE.

He determines the number of stars
and calls them each by name.

PSALM 147:4

DO YOU REMEMBER AS A CHILD, shuffling out into the backyard on a warm August night in your pajamas and fuzzy slippers to watch the Perseid meteor shower? Tiny specks of dust, most no bigger than a grain of sand, roar into the atmosphere at speeds of 132,000 mph, lighting up the summer sky in a brilliant display of what we kids used to call shooting stars. Not one or two, but hundreds! It's one of nature's most amazing spectacles—if the conditions are right for viewing.

You'll have a hard time seeing them if you are near a big city, and of course we usually can't see them at all in Seattle, where we live, because it's likely to be raining or at least a bit overcast. But if you're standing on a remote hillside outside your tent in the middle of Mongolia, halfway between Ulaanbaatar and Kharakhorum, the view is pretty remarkable. So it was for me, as I huddled with my family under a canopy of stars and witnessed a display of God's handiwork unlike any, I daresay, we will ever see again. And to think that most people probably missed it, not because they didn't want to see it but because other things—streetlamps, city lights, rainclouds—got in the way.

That happens to me too; I let unimportant things get in the way of what's really significant. I see small, hungry children, like those we found living in tunnels under the streets of the capital city of Mongolia, and I am certain that I will never forget their thin little bodies or the look in their eyes. I determine to always remember their stories—of how, homeless and abandoned, they sought shelter from the freezing temperatures of the harsh Mongolian winters by living underground in tunnels dug to house the steam pipes that run beneath the city. But then I inadvertently let other things get in the way. When I return home from my travels and life resumes

Illuminated huts against a star-filled sky in Turkana, Kenya.

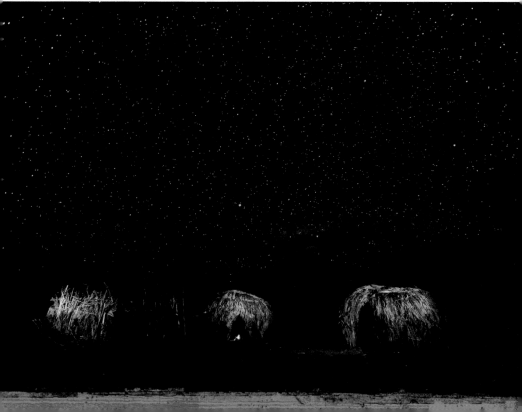

The Cristo de la Concordia (Christ of Peace), high above Cochabamba, Bolivia, reminds us that God invites us to join Him in caring for the world.

its normally hectic pace, I find it harder and harder to remember their faces. Just like the Perseid meteor shower, hidden by city lights, those precious children are too easily obscured by a busy life filled with daily demands, by activities that in the moment seem so important but in the larger scheme of things really aren't.

Yet, even though I don't see them in my mind's eye, the children are still there. And when the conditions are just right, when my heart is quiet, attentive to the prompting of God's Holy Spirit, I can see their faces as if it were yesterday. It turns out that in the same way God numbered the stars and calls them by name, He calls my name too. If I listen carefully enough, I can hear His still, small voice inviting me to join Him in caring for those He loves.

—Reneé